T0208268

# KIA:
## KILLED IN the ALAMO
A Saga of Travis,Bonham,Bowie,Crockett and
The Other Brave Defenders of The Alamo

ROY SULLIVAN

authorHOUSE®

AuthorHouse™
1663 Liberty Drive
Bloomington, IN 47403
www.authorhouse.com
Phone: 1 (800) 839-8640

© 2019 Roy Sullivan. All rights reserved.

No part of this book may be reproduced, stored in a retrieval system, or
transmitted by any means without the written permission of the author.

Published by AuthorHouse  07/09/2019

ISBN: 978-1-7283-1862-2 (sc)
ISBN: 978-1-7283-1861-5 (e)

Print information available on the last page.

Any people depicted in stock imagery provided by Getty Images are models,
and such images are being used for illustrative purposes only.
Certain stock imagery © Getty Images.

This book is printed on acid-free paper.

Because of the dynamic nature of the Internet, any web addresses or links contained in
this book may have changed since publication and may no longer be valid. The views
expressed in this work are solely those of the author and do not necessarily reflect the
views of the publisher, and the publisher hereby disclaims any responsibility for them.

Colonel Travis' final speech to his Alamo defenders:

"Within a few days—perhaps in a very few hours—we must all be in eternity. This is our destiny and we cannot avoid it. This is our certain doom.

"I have deceived you long by the promise of help. But I crave your pardon. In deceiving you, I also deceived myself, having first being deceived by others."

(as recalled by Private Louis Moses Rose, the sole Alamo combatant who escaped and survived)

For Nancy: Editor, Critic, Photographer, Co-conspirator

# CONTENTS

# ILLUSTRATIONS

William B. Travis of South Carolina: Commander of the Alamo and the First Texas Casualty as the Mexican Assault Began March 6, 1836. Credit N.K. Rogers photograph

# ONE

## TRAVIS ARRIVES

IT WAS A chilly, windy February 3 and the insipid breeze rattled the window panes throughout San Antonio, also called Bexar, in Texas. The sky, a dark, ominous grey, foretold snow for South Texas.

It was a busy day for just-arrived Lieutenant Colonel William Barret Travis and his thirty dirty, tired companions adding to the paltry strength of the former mission—now crumbling fortress—called the Alamo.

Texas Governor Smith ordered Travis and his regulars to reinforce the Alamo garrison much to Travis's chagrin. He minced no words in an immediate request back to the Governor:

> *I beg that Your Excellency will recall the order for me to go to Bexar in command of so few men. I am willing, nay anxious, to go to the defense of Bexar, and I have done everything in my power to equip the enlisted men and get them off. But, Sir, I am unwilling to risk my reputation (which is ever dear to a volunteer) by going off into the enemy's country with so little, so few men, and those so badly equipped— the fact there is no necessity for my services to command these few men. The company officers will be amply sufficient.*

Roy Sullivan

Staring out the narrow window of his new Alamo quarters in its west wall, Travis was discouraged. Governor Smith failed to reply to Travis' request for relief. Not only that, another Lieutenant Colonel, James C. Neill, already commanded the Alamo garrison of which Travis and his thirty men were just a new portion.

"Trouble comes in threes," Travis muttered to himself, remembering there was a third "colonel" in the Alamo—the famed knife-fighter Jim Bowie—who headed another group of thirty loyal, rowdy, hard-drinking volunteers.

Adding to his worries, Travis had just received a report from the fort's quartermaster, Lieutenant Eliel Melton, about the meager supply of provisions, gun powder and lead available to defend their crumbling fortress against the entire Mexican army.

Their opponent, soon to arrive in Texas, was the much larger, professional army led by General-in-Chief Antonio Lopez de Santa Ana, who was also President of Mexico.

Santa Ana was on his way north, some said he had already crossed the Rio Grande River and heading north for Bexar (note: also spelled Bejar) with several thousand troops. His probable intentions were to seize the Alamo and terrorize Texas inhabitants all the way to the Sabine River separating Texas and Louisiana. A disciplinary lesson was due those ungrateful Texans and Santa Ana would administer it.

Travis' adjutant, Captain John Baugh, rapped on the open door, announcing, "Officer to see you, Colonel."

"Who?"

"A new lieutenant named Bonham. Know him, sir?"

Baugh's reply immediately lifted Travis's spirits.

"Jim Bonham! Come in! Of course I know him! We're both from South Carolina!"

A tall, dark haired man, grinning broadly, stepped into the office and saluted.

"Lieutenant Bonham reporting for duty, Sir!"

Stepping around the desk, Travis returned the salute and gripped the younger man's hand.

"Good to see you, Jim! Understand you've been traipsing around San Felipe and Goliad!

"Sit down, sit down," Travis pointed to the cane chair in front of his desk.

"Had your coffee yet?" Without waiting for an answer, Travis called, "Joe! Bring our pot and cups!"

The coffee pot was still hot so Travis' servant, a slave named Joe, quickly provided cups and the dark brew.

"This is Joe, my manservant," Travis introduced him. "Joe, this is Lieutenant Bonham, another South Carolinian."

"Are you from South Carolina, too, Joe?" Bonham asked.

Already on his way out the door, Joe turned and grinned. "No, suh. I was born in old Kentuck."

Blowing on his coffee cup, Travis studied the young officer. "Now, tell me how you happened to come to Texas, to this very same destination as myself, all the way from South Carolina."

"Well, sir…"

"We're both South Carolinians. Call me Buck, Jim."

"Yes, sir. Thank you… Buck.

"Not much to tell…even less to brag about. I enrolled at South Carolina College in '24, got kicked out for causing a ruckus. Next I studied law and opened a tiny office in Pendleton in the thirties. Also worked for South Carolina Governor Hamilton during that nullification problem. After that died down, I returned to my law practice."

Travis chuckled, extending long legs under the desk. "Yep, I remember hearing about your little court fracas, defending a female client. Got you jailed for a spell by that court judge, didn't it?"

Bonham, nodded. "Yes, sir…"

"Buck, remember?"

"You remember correctly, Buck. I caned the opposing attorney who disparaged my client right there in that very courtroom. The judge wasn't amused and sentenced me to 90 days in jail for my chivalric display."

The younger officer grinned at the memory. "It made me famous with all the local ladies for a spell, until I met one who spurned me despite my short-lived fame."

Travis leaned forward. "What decided you to come to Texas?"

"By then I was in Alabama and heard about what the Mexicans were trying to do to you folks here in Texas. Several of us wrote a citizens' resolution to Sam Houston expressing our strong feeling and support. The next logical step seemed to recruit armed volunteers to go to Texas and offer our services—not just words—to Sam Houston…"

Travis interrupted. "And the militia you dubbed the Mobile Greys was the result?"

"Exactly. You are very well informed, Buck."

"Next, you accompanied those same Mobile Greys to San Antonio?"

Bonham frowned. "Yes, sir, but we didn't make it to San Antonio and the Alamo until the Mexican army, under General Cos, already was retreating to Mexico with its tail between its legs. I also wrote Sam Houston on December 1, offering my services without compensation—-like rations, land or pay."

Travis grinned broadly. "And did he take you up on your offer?"

"Yes, sir. I was commissioned a Second Lieutenant of cavalry that same month."

Travis whistled. "Congratulations! I also heard he recommended you be promoted all the way to Major. Didn't he?"

Bonham looked at his boots in embarrassment. "Yes, sir."

Travis enjoyed the younger man's discomfort. "I also heard

he wrote that your 'influence in the army is great, more so than those who would be generals."

Bonham swallowed. "I don't know about that, sir." He studied his boots again.

"I'm mighty glad you're here, Jim. The Mexicans must be kept out of East Texas and our position here is key to that."

Nodding his head, Bonham added softly, "Yes, sir. I realize the importance of the Alamo in keeping Texas independent."

Travis struck the desk with his fist. "Too bad lots of your Greys headed south to Goliad where they tied up with Colonel Fannin at La Bahia. Fannin thinks his Fort Defiance at Goliad/La Bahia will be the first target for the Mexicans."

Bonham gestured. "Colonel Bowie convinced me this is the place to take our stand. He showed me on a map how the Alamo blocks the way into East Texas. I'm honored to serve with you, Colonel."

"Here," Travis lifted a paper from the desk which he had read minutes before Bonham's entrance. "Listen to this, a letter Jim Bowie sent Governor Smith just yesterday:

> *The salvation of Texas depends in great measure on keeping Bexar out of the hands of the enemy. It serves as the frontier picquet guard, and if it were in the possession of Santa Ana, there is no stronghold from which to repel him in his march toward the Sabine.*"

Travis slapped his desk again after reading aloud the copy of Bowie's letter. "So we're all agreed! The Alamo must be held at all costs!"

Travis paused. "I've a question for you, Jim. What have been your duties since you and Colonel Bowie reported for duty here?"

Bonham grinned. "Although I was commissioned a lieutenant in the Texas Cavalry, I've been working for Captain

Dickinson, your artillery chief. Seems your dozen or so cannon will be more important than cavalry when those Mexicans get here and surround the Alamo."

Smile gone, Travis clasped his hands. "The news isn't all good. I've heard several reports…some of them just rumors…that Santa Ana and several thousand soldiers already are heading our way. *Not* (italics added) to Goliad when Colonel Fannin is comfortably established with over three hundred men and lots of artillery."

Travis added with a grin. "I'm an artilleryman, too. I was commissioned a lieutenant colonel in the artillery.

"Our mission here is to prepare the Alamo to defeat the attack we expect from Santa Ana. We need to recruit more men, a subject at which you're already handy. More provisions, weapons, ammunition—everything's needed—and in a hurry! Even these ancient Alamo walls need strengthening. The Mexicans have artillery, too, and they'll try to blow us out of these old fortifications.

"Jim, I'm tickled you're already working with Captain Dickinson and his cannon cockers. Learn as much as you can from them. You're right about the superiority of the cannon over the cavalry saber in our circumstances."

Travis leaned forward, face to face with Bonham. "Even though we are soldiers, there's a political angle I must mention. Sam Houston is our commander-in-chief but he must contend with the Governor, Henry Smith. Some of the delegates to the Texas Convention at Washington-on-the-Brazos, are attempting to replace Governor Smith with Lieutenant Governor Robinson. I might as well tell you, Colonel Fannin, down in Goliad, sides with the Lieutenant Governor.

"Just remember, despite the political turmoil, our job is to blunt Santa Ana's attack on South Texas and prevent his terrorizing the settlers in East Texas."

"I've taken enough of your time, Colonel." Bonham stood.

"Just wanted to introduce myself and assure you that a South Carolina Red Bank neighbor is at your service. More than a neighbor, you and I may even be distantly related!"

Captain Baugh was at the door again. "Our engineer, Major Green Jameson, is here, Colonel, to take you on an inspection of our fortifications."

"I'll be right there." Travis upset his coffee while standing,

"Already I'm asking you to do something for me, Jim, in addition to working for Captain Dickinson. Since we have artillery emplaced all along our entire perimeter, you'll have occasion to visit and work with all those teams. I'd appreciate your sharing with me your impressions of our garrison morale. Thanks for coming by...return at any time.

"Now let's get to work!"

James B. Bonham of South Carolina: Faithful Courier and Kinsman of Travis. Despite Bonham's Pleas, Fannin Twice Denied Aid for the Alamo. Credit N.K. Rogers photograph

# TWO

## THE ALAMO

**E**STABLISHED BY THE Franciscans in 1719 as a mission to convert local Indians to Christianity, the Alamo's full name was Mission San Antonio de Valero. Later the mission was called simply the Alamo, meaning poplar tree in Spanish.

The chapel or church is the best known, best preserved and smallest part of the original mission. The chapel sits on the southeast extremity of the sprawling, now long-gone structure. The chapel was the best fortified element of the mission. Its stone walls were about five feet thick and twenty-two and one half feet tall. There was no roof on the chapel.

Immediately beside the chapel was a large garden containing water wells. Their location made the conversion of the garden into cattle and horse pens logical.

Adjoining the chapel was a rectangular structure encircling the cattle pens, the garden/courtyard, the "long" barracks and hospital. The adobe walls of the barracks and hospital were about sixteen and one half feet tall and three feet thick.

The remainder of the original mission occupied the most area. It was a long, narrow rectangular courtyard bordered on the south end by a large main gate within the smaller or "low" barracks.

The interior sides of this larger rectangle of approximately two acres consisted of one-story adobe rooms, some covered by thatched roofs. The exterior walls were some eight feet tall and about three feet wide.

Earth ramps led to several parapets atop the tall outer walls. These were strong points, armed with one or more of the twenty-one cannon available to the Alamo defenders. The outer walls of the rectangle were limestone, adobe and mortar. The narrow ends of the rectangle were about 60 feet wide. A small stream trickled through it from northwest to southwest.

The long west wall of the mission faced the San Antonio River. On the other side of the river was the town, San Antonio de Bexar (or Bejar). At the time the town was simply called Bexar. (locally pronounced "Bear.")

Although far from being impregnable (Santa Ana referred to it as a "fortress" in his later victorious after-action report to Mexico City) the Alamo's defenses, adequately manned, could withstand medium-scale assaults.

Travis assessed the defensibility of the Alamo in one of his many letters requesting assistance:

"...with 200 more men I believe this place can be maintained & I hope they will be sent to us as soon as possible."

Without the requested assistance, Travis was unequivocal.

"Yet should we receive no reinforcements, I am determined to defend it to the last, and should Bejar fall, your friend will be buried beneath its ruins."

Roy Sullivan

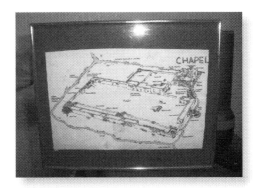

Sketch of the Alamo Which Travis Vowed to Defend to the Last. Credit N.K. Rogers photograph

One Alamo area which seemed the easiest penetrable thus hardest to defend was a small fenced or "palisaded" but otherwise open area between the chapel's southwest corner and the intersecting west wall and main gate. This was the defensive position later assigned by Travis to the indomitable Davy Crockett (another "Colonel") and his "twelve boys" from Tennessee.

This was clearly the least defensible position in the old mission: 115 feet of open space between the southwest corner of the chapel and the two-story building containing the main gate and the "low" barracks.

At the front of the palisaded area was an eight foot high fence of cedar timbers, set six feet apart. Outside the fence was a two-foot high bank of earth from which riflemen could fire. Before the unfinished front trench was a barrier of felled, buried trees with their sharpened trunks facing outward. Midway in the palisade was a four-pound cannon positioned to fire through an opening.

These were the fortifications and features of the Alamo of which Jim Bowie pledged to Governor Smith: "we will rather die in these ditches than give them up to the enemy."

His pledge would become a prophecy.

Jim Bowie of Kentucky: Famous Knife Fighter and Commander of the Alamo's Volunteers, Bedridden Before and During the Final Assault. Credit N.K. Rogers photograph

# THREE

## JIM BOWIE

COLONEL JAMES BOWIE was no newcomer to Texas and its struggle as were Travis and Bonham. He joined forces with Lieutenant Colonel Neill, the current commander of the Alamo garrison, on January 1. Six foot Bowie, the Kentuckian famous for his dueling, drinking, exploits and knife-fighting, settled in San Antonio in 1828, long before Bonham or Travis arrived. Bowie became a Roman Catholic, a Mexican citizen, and married a daughter of the rich and powerful Veramendi family of San Antonio. They were married in the San Fernando Church whose bell-ringing later announced the approach of the Mexican army. Bowie became a prominent and respected leader of the Bexar community. Elected a colonel in the militia by 100 supporters on July 13, 1835, he used that title for the rest of his life.

The Bowie knife, designed by his brother, Rezin, had a large, single-edged nine inch blade and blade guard. Part of its back edge was turned to a sharp point.

Of the famous knife, Colonel David Crockett wrote:

"Colonel Bowie had occasion to draw his famous knife, and I wish I may be shot if the bare sight of it wasn't enough to give a man of a squeamish stomach the colic. He saw I was admiring it and said 'Colonel, you might tickle a fellow's ribs a long time with this little instrument before you'd make him laugh!"

12

Bowie's wife, the nineteen year old, blonde Maria Ursula de Veramendi Bowie, later bore them two children. While on an 1833 business trip to Mississippi, Bowie received the tragic news that his wife, their two children, her mother and father had died of cholera in Monclova, Mexico. Bowie had taken them there, a cooler environment, to avoid the epidemic. Depressed and despondent, he returned to Bexar/San Antonio, living with his two sisters-in-law at the Veramendi home.

So Bowie was a Texan by inclination, a Mexican by citizenship and a Catholic by choice. He was fluent in Spanish and an ardent supporter of independence for Texas.

Bowie had a long association with the Alamo, having laid siege to its occupation by Mexican General Cos. South of town at Mission Concepcion, Bowie, Juan Seguin and Jim Fannin plus ninety-two volunteers took defensive positions near the old mission.

Mexican General Cos, brother-in-law of General Santa Ana, quickly acted on his scouts' reports concerning the Texans' movements. He dispatched some 475 troops of the Morales Division. This division, known as the "Invincibles" contained infantry, cavalry and a six-pound cannon.

Despite an early morning fog on October 28, 1835, Cos ordered an attack against the Bowie/Fannin/Seguin force positioned on a curve of the San Antonio River. The Texans' defensive position was ideal. The approaching Mexican soldiers were easily visible advancing toward the Texans crouching behind a small embankment. This embankment allowed the Texans to partially show themselves, pick and fire at a target, scramble down to safety, reload their muskets, and repeat the process again and again.

Texas rifleman Noah Smithwick described the ensuing carnage:

"Our long rifles—and I thought I never heard rifles crack so keen, after the roar of the (Mexican) cannon—mowed down the Mexicans at a rate that might well have made braver hearts…recoil. Three times they charged, but there was a platoon to receive them. Three times we picked off their gunners, the last one with a lighted match in his hand; then a panic seized them, and they broke. They jumped on the mules attached to the cannon, two or three to a mule, without even taking time to cut them loose, and struck out for the fort (the Alamo), leaving the loaded gun on the field. With a ringing cheer we mounted the bank and gave chase. We turned their cannon on them, adding wings to their flight. They dropped their muskets, and splashing through the shallow water of the river, fled helter-skelter as if pursued by all the furies."

The initial Mexican attack failed due to the accuracy of Texan musket fire but the Mexicans tried three more times before retiring back to San Antonio. Mexican losses were ten dead and the abandoned six-pound cannon. One Texan (Richard Andrews) was mortally wounded and another injured. People living in the town reported the actual Mexican losses were seventy-five killed and wounded.

Bowie added to his combat credentials later at the little-known "Grass Fight." On November 26, a scout reported that a Mexican pack train, guarded by 150 *soldados*, was approaching Bexar with needed supplies. Rumors among the Texans were that the "supplies" was actually a silver payroll for the Mexican troops. Bowie set out with 40 cavalrymen to intercept it and found the pack train approximately one mile from Bexar. Impetuous Bowie ordered an immediate charge, despite knowing his supporting infantry was well behind him. Although outnumbered three to one, Bowie's men charged the Mexicans, who were being reinforced at that same moment from Bexar. Routed, the Mexicans withdrew into town, leaving the pack mules behind.

Bowie's eager troops opened the packs, hunting for the expected silver—but found only fodder intended for the army animals in Bexar. Seventeen Mexican soldiers were killed or wounded. Texas losses were four wounded, all members of Lieutenant Salvador Flores' unit.

Bowie received a January 18 letter from Major General Sam Houston, commander of the Texas army, giving him the option to demolish the Alamo and move its troops and artillery to Gonzales and Copano.

Houston thought highly of Bowie, praising him as follows. "There is no man on whose forecast, prudence and valor I place a higher estimate."

Despite this accolade, Bowie (and Neill) decided not to demolish or abandon the Alamo. At the time, Houston was busy negotiating a peace agreement with the Cherokee Indians with whom he once lived.

Bowie and Neill set to work improving the old mission's defenses. Bowie set his thirty intensively loyal, hard-drinking volunteers to work under Engineer Green Jameson to strengthen walls and build gun emplacements. Neill's men worked just as hard to ready the defenses, gather and store provisions—including cattle—for the assault that was sure and soon to come.

Bowie also sought support from the fledgling, struggling Texas Convention, warning: "Relief at this post in men, money and provisions is of vital importance *and is wanted instantly.*" (italics added)

Three colonels at the Alamo: Lieutenant Colonel Neill, the nominal commander of the garrison; Lieutenant Colonel Travis, the newly-arrived, second-in-command; and Colonel Bowie, acknowledged leader of his thirty, intensely loyal volunteers.

Roy Sullivan

The Alamo was about to gain a fourth.

Davy Crockett of Tennessee: Famous Frontiersman and Advocate of Texas Independence. Credit N.K. Rogers photograph

# FOUR
## DAVY CROCKETT ARRIVES

CROCKETT LOST HIS Tennessee reelection to Congress in 1835, probably influenced by President of the U.S. Andrew Jackson's animosity toward him. Soured by his political defeat, he looked for other ways to support his family. Giant, mysterious Texas appealed to everyone's imagination. Stories—some true, some false—about the opportunities, vastness of fertile lands and possible riches to be made induced his decision to pack up and GTT (Gone To Texas).

On February 8, 1836, thirteen Tennesseans rode into Bexar. Although their numbers were small, their reputation as the "Tennessee Mounted Volunteers" was well-known, mostly because of their leader, the acclaimed Colonel David (Davy) Crockett. He had been elected a lieutenant colonel of the 57th Regiment of Militia back in Tennessee. As was common, the title stuck with him for life.

In the Main Plaza of San Antonio, Crockett greeted the admiring citizenry and, as he often did, gave a speech reiterating his many stories about mountain life and ending with what he had told his former constituents back home on his departure.

"You can all go to hell; I'm going to Texas!"

The crowd went wild. In a quick change of tone, he told the assembled crowd:

"I have come to your country, though not, I hope, with any selfish motive whatever. I have come to aid you all that I can in our noble cause. I shall identify myself with your interests, and all the honour that I desire is that of defending as a *high private* (italics added), in common with my fellow citizens, the liberties of our common country."

The crowd was jubilant, but even more so at the quickly organized January 10 fandango/dance celebration held that night in honor of Crockett's arrival. All the local ladies were invited to mix with the Alamo defenders/volunteers (now totaling 142) and town people. The party lasted all night, so it was still going at one o'clock the next morning, when word came that Santa Ana's army was indeed on the move toward Bexar/ San Antonio, the Alamo being its target. When the message was handed Travis, Bowie and Crockett, it created little concern among them. They decided the Mexicans were still far away.

The message was from patriot Placido Benavides and his Tejano (Texans of Mexican heritage favoring independence) company scouting the Mexican army somewhere south of the Rio Grande River. He wrote:

"At this moment, I have received a very certain notice that the commander-in-chief, Antonio Lopez de Santa Ana, marches for the city of San Antonio to take possession thereof, with 3,000 men."

Not included in the Travis/Bowie/Crockett huddle was Lieutenant Colonel James C. Neill, present commander of the Alamo. He would depart the next morning on twenty days leave because of urgent family problems. No one expected Neill to return, especially Neill.

Who would replace Neill as commander of the Alamo? Would it be twenty-six year old Lieutenant Colonel Travis;

the renowned, forty-nine year old Colonel Bowie; or the just-arrived "High Private" Colonel Crockett, fifty-nine years of age?"

A drunken Bowie helped solve the problem by accosting several town people and ordering the release of all prisoners from the local jail on January 13. Chagrinned, Travis was quick to write Governor Smith that same day of Bowie's misconduct.

"I am unwilling to be responsible for the drunken irregularities of any man." Travis described Bowie's actions in detail, ending Travis would leave his post immediately were it not for the importance of the Alamo:

"It is more important to occupy this post than I imagined when I last saw you. It is the key to Texas…"

Once the drinks wore off, a seriously ill (probably with typhoid) Bowie was willing to compromise with Travis. Bowie would command the garrison's volunteers, who readily elected him their leader. Travis would command the regulars and the volunteer cavalry. The two colonels even cooperated on a letter to Governor Smith about their new arrangement. They could not neglect another warning to Governor Smith:

"There is no doubt that the enemy will shortly advance upon this place, and that this will be the first point of attack. We must therefore urge the necessity of sending reinforcements as speedily as possible to our aid."

It would not to be the last plea from the Alamo for assistance.

Roy Sullivan

General Antonio Lopez de Santa Ana, General-in-Chief of the Mexican army and President of Mexico, Ordered the Massacre of all Alamo Captured Defenders. Credit N.K. Rogers photograph

# FIVE

## SANTA ANA IS COMING!
## SANTA ANA IS COMING!

I N MEXICO CITY, General Santa Ana was enraged with the reports being received from his northern-most province, Texas. Upon hearing of the defeat of General Martin Perfecto de Cos, his brother-in-law, he ordered his "Army of Operations" to conduct a punitive expedition against Texas.

On the way north, he encountered the remnants of Cos' battered force heading south. Santa Ana was livid. Here was his brother-in-law, another general officer in the Mexican army, defeated and paroled back to Mexico by those ragtag Texan rebels.

Santa Ana ordered Cos to turn around his 800 bedraggled, hungry, some wounded, men and accompany Santa Ana back to Bexar to seize the Alamo and punish anyone opposing him.

To instill in all troops, particularly those of Cos, with the necessary warlike attitude, Santa Ana issued the following proclamation:

"Companions in Arms! Our sacred duties have conducted us to these plains, and urge us forward to combat with that mob of ungrateful adventurers on whom our authorities have incautiously lavished favors which they failed to bestow on Mexicans. They have appropriated to themselves our territories, and have raised the standard of rebellion, in order that this fertile and expanded department may be detached from our Republic; persuading themselves that our unfortunate dissentions have incapacitated us for the defense of our native lands. Wretches! They will soon see their folly.

"Soldiers! Your comrades have been treacherously sacrificed at Anahuac, Goliad, and Bejar; and you are the men chosen to *chastise the assassins.* (italics added)

"My Friends! We will march to the spot whether we are called by the interests of the nation in whose services we are engaged. The candidates for "acres" of land in Texas will learn to their sorrow, that their auxiliaries from New Orleans, Mobile, Boston, New York, and other northern ports (from whence no aid ought to proceed) are insignificant, and that the Mexicans, though naturally generous, will not suffer outrages with impunity—injurious and dishonorable to their country— let the perpetrators be whom they may."

The gregarious Colonel Crockett made frequent visits to town from the Alamo, conversing with families hurriedly carting their possessions through San Antonio and east toward Louisiana to avoid the coming war.

From one traveler, Crockett learned that forward elements of Santa Ana's army were already near Leon Creek, just a few miles away from Bexar. He immediately shared the news with Travis who posted a sentinel in the tall belfry of the San Fernando Church (the same church in which Bowie was married) in the center of town, to watch for any sign of the Mexicans.

As the glistening symbol and center of the growing town (San Antonio/Bexar) the tower provided a panoramic view of the neighboring countryside.

The sentinel repeatedly rang the church bell on February 23 as he sighted the approaching Mexican army.

Colonel Travis was cautious. To double check the alarm,

Travis sent two riders, Doctor John Sutherland (who was unable to definitely identify Bowie's illness) and J.W. Smith. Less than two miles away from town, the two riders doubled back at full speed. They ran into the advance elements of the Mexican army, turned around and raced back to Travis.

Panic seized the town folk. Some stayed in their homes while others hurriedly packed-up and headed east. Soldiers not already inside the Alamo marched toward the old mission past young ladies waving handkerchiefs in farewell. It was a somber scene since the ladies thought the soldiers would not survive the coming battle. Another prophecy!

Captain Juan Seguin, Tejano (a Texan of Mexican ancestry), a stanch independence supporter and officer in the Texas army, remembered his troops filing down the streets and into the Alamo:

"As we marched Portrero Street (now called Commerce), the ladies wailed 'Poor fellows! You will all be killed! What shall we do?'"

As his troops entered Bexar/San Antonio, Santa Ana hoisted a red flag atop the San Fernando Church where Travis' sentinel previously had rung the alarm. The red flag reminded Mexican troops that no prisoners would be taken.

Travis, as well as others sheltered inside the Alamo walls, scoffed at the red flag meaning death to all defenders.

Travis' options were to fight a much superior enemy, surrender to him or somehow escape his encirclement. According to Mexican Lieutenant de la Pena, whose detailed writings are often quoted by historians, Travis' men urged him to surrender because of their lack of food and munitions. Travis delayed a decision, initially expecting more relief such as the 32 just-arrived men from Gonzales. Eventually, Travis announced his decision: if no relief had arrived by March 5, he would surrender or let the garrison try to escape during the night.

If the symbolism of the red flag atop the San Fernando was not clear enough, Santa Ana issued another order to his army:

"Now, this is very important and is to be stressed in any pronouncement we make. Any foreigner in Tejas (Texas) who is arrested while in possession of arms of any kind is to be judged a pirate and treated accordingly. Finally…once the battle begins, if the enemy has not previously surrendered, no prisoners will be taken. *They are to be shot on the battlefield where we capture them.*" (italics added)

Among the reasons for Santa Ana's anger at the upstart Texans may have been his own narrow escapes. He was reportedly incensed when he was almost struck by a long-range shot from a musket, probably fired at him by Davy Crockett from an Alamo parapet. Anther reason was that the house in which he was staying was struck by a cannon shot from the Alamo.

General-in-Chief and President Santa Ana did not spend all his time reconnoitering and planning how to defeat the Texans in the Alamo. Mexican First Sergeant Francisco Becerras of the Matamoros Battalion related the following:

"While searching for timbers to construct a bridge for the assault on the Alamo, General Manuel Castrillon entered a house and found there a lady and her beautiful daughter. Castrillon told Santa Ana about the encounter and the latter was in a 'great fever' to see the daughter. He commanded the lady and daughter be brought to his quarters in the town. Castrillon refused, saying it was not a military matter. It fell on General Jose Minon to comply with Santa Ana's order. He dutifully delivered the message to the mother.

"The mother replied with a definite no. She was not only a respectable woman but the widow of an officer who had commanded a company in the Mexican army. Moreover, she was of a good family and had always conducted herself with propriety. Santa Ana was not her president and couldn't get her daughter except by marriage.

"Minon, eager to please, volunteered to Santa Ana that he had in his command a man who was capable of impersonating a priest. The latter agreed to perform a fake ceremony in Santa Ana's quarters. And so the 'ceremony' was held in late February in the midst of the Alamo campaign. Later, the deceived and trusting young lady was sent to San Luis Potosi in the carriage of General Minon…I do not know when she ascertained that Gen. Santa Ana was already a married man, and the father of a family, and that she had been made victim of a foul and rascally plot."

Accompanying many of the Alamo defenders were their families moving into the mission for protection. Among them was the wife of Gregorio Esperanza and their four children. Other family members fleeing to the Alamo were Juana Losoya Melton, wife of Eliel Melton, the Alamo's quartermaster, and Juanita's mother, Concepcion Losoya and two sons. Others may have included "Madame Candelaria," wife of Candelario Villanueva, a member of Captain Seguin's Tejano company.

Madame Candelaria claimed to have nursed Jim Bowie during his long illness which took him out of action in February, even confining him to his cot during the eventual Mexican assault.

On February 26, Crockett wrote in his journal the following:

"Colonel Bowie has been taken sick from overexertion and exposure. He did not leave his bed today until twelve o'clock. He is worth a dozen common men in a situation like ours."

Madame Candaleria gave a peculiar description of the famed Davy Crockett. "He was one of the strangest-looking men I ever saw. He had the face of a woman and his manner was that of a young girl."

Among other women in the Alamo were Susannah Dickinson, wife of artillery officer, Captain Almeron Dickinson (also spelled Almaron Dickerson), and her daughter Angelina; Juana Navarro Alsbury, the wife of Doctor Horatio Alsbury; and Gertrudis Navarro, Juana's sister. Both Alsbury and Navarro were cousins of Bowie's deceased wife, Ursula. Mrs. Alsbury went to the Alamo to care for Bowie, casting doubt about Madame Candelaria's claimed presence or duties there.

The next day, February 24, the opposing forces settled down for a long siege. Several of Santa Ana's generals presumed the siege eventually would result in the starvation/capitulation of the Alamo's defenders with few casualties to their own troops. Santa Ana had other plans, as evinced by the above general order about the execution of prisoners, and the hoisting of the blood red flag on the San Fernando Church.

Seriously ill, Bowie was bed ridden. Travis became the sole commander of the Alamo. As such he penned his most famous letter:

"To the People of Texas & All Americans in the world:

I am besieged by a thousand or more of the Mexicans under Santa Ana. I have sustained a continual Bombardment and cannonade for 24 hours and have not lost a man. The enemy has demanded a surrender at discretion, or otherwise, the garrison are to be put to the sword, if the fort is taken. I have answered the demand with a cannon shot, & our flag still waves proudly from the walls. I shall never surrender or retreat. Then, I call on you in the name of Liberty, of patriotism &

everything dear to the American character, to come to our aid, with all dispatch. The enemy is receiving reinforcements daily and will not doubt increase to three or four thousand in four or five days. If this call is neglected, I am determined to sustain myself as long as possible & die like a soldier who never forgets what is due to his own honor and that of his country.

Victory or Death (underlined)
William Barret Travis, Lt. Col. Comdt

P.S. The Lord is on our side. When the enemy appeared in sight we had not three bushels of corn. We have since found in deserted houses 80-90 bushels and got into the walls 20 or 30 head of Beeves."

# SIX
## COUNTLESS APPEALS

**A**LTHOUGH TRAVIS' HIGHLY compelling letter was read and discussed by Texans "& All Americans in the world," he penned and dispatched many more appeals for assistance and reinforcements, most of which were unanswered.

Among the earliest of these was the February 14 letter to Texas Governor Smith, jointly written by both Bowie and Travis. Having compromised their command differences, they wrote:

"There is no doubt that the enemy will shortly advance upon this place, and that this will be the first point of attack. We must therefore urge the necessity of sending reinforcements *as speedily as possible to our aid.*" (italics added)

Days later, on February 18, Travis dispatched a plea for help directly to Fannin at Goliad/La Bahia/Fort Defiance via his trusted friend, Lieutenant Bonham. The latter was not only a former South Carolina neighbor of Travis but a second cousin as well. He was an organizer of the Mobile Greys, a company of Alabama volunteers, now members of Fannin's large garrison of over 400 men at Goliad/La Bahia/Fort Defiance.

It is not known if Travis specifically ordered Bonham to return with his report about Fannin's intentions. Bonham certainly promised Travis a report on his own, due to their friendship and ties.

Once with Fannin at Goliad, Bonham probably began by outlining the Alamo's shortage of men and material. Fannin countered that his own garrison, Goliad, was equally imperiled by Mexican General Urrea's advancing columns coming up the Gulf coast.

Goliad cannot be abandoned, Fannin ranted, since it is the critical link with Copano, a key point of the frontier. Fannin probably bragged that—being the "senior officer on the frontier and responsible to Lieutenant Governor Robinson" (who was attempting to oust Governor Smith)—he could not assist Travis at the Alamo.

Bonham ended his plea to Fannin and his men with:

"What we need now is for every fighting man in this part of Texas to rush to the Alamo. Strengthen our perimeters! Give us help! The freedom of Texas and the whole United States lies in the balance. Help us!"

Fannin sat, toying with the pommel of his saber, during Bonham's presentation. Finally, he looked up and smiled at the young lieutenant, grimy and disheveled from his long, hazardous first ride through the Mexican lines surrounding the Alamo.

"I'll think it over," Fannin stood, ending the conversation.

Angry at the response, Bonham remounted his horse and spurred the tired animal onward to Victoria where he repeated his plea to a group of farmers. On his horse again, Bonham headed for Gonzales where he was sure to find relief for the Alamo. There on August 1, he found mostly women and children, the men being rounded up by George Kimball for a foray through the Mexican lines to the Alamo. Kimball's group would later be immortalized as the "Magnificent 32."

Meanwhile, back at the Alamo, Travis dispatched 19-year old Ben Highsmith before Santa Ana's complete encirclement of the town. Highsmith was bound for Goliad to again appeal to Fannin for reinforcements.

On Highsmith's arrival, Fannin turned down the request to assist Travis. Highsmith jumped back on his horse and rode away. Shortly thereafter he was discovered and hotly pursued by Mexican cavalry but eventually made his way safely to Gonzales. There he ran into another messenger, newly-arrived Lieutenant Bonham. Highsmith recounted his narrow escape and warned that the Mexican army now surrounded and controlled San Antonio/Bexar and the neighboring area.

Highsmith argued for some time, trying to dissuade Bonham from trying to return to the Alamo:

"We'll wait and join the volunteers from San Felipe and other places. It's near impossible to get through the Mexican lines right now."

Bonham frowned and shook his head. "I will report the result of my mission to Travis or die in the attempt."

The next morning, March 2, Bonham said farewell, crossed the Guadalupe River and headed for the encircled Alamo. He was determined to keep that commitment to his friend, compatriot and kinsman, Will Travis.

Meanwhile, Travis had written a February 23 letter, this one initially addressed to Andrew Ponton, Judge of Gonzales. Then he changed the address "To any of the inhabitants of Texas."

Travis handed the letter to Dr. Sutherland for delivery to Gonzales. It was terse:

"The enemy in large force is in sight. We want men and provisions. Send them to us. We have 150 men and are determined to defend the Alamo to the last. Give us assistance."

Sutherland injured his knee when his horse previously fell on him, but he was in the saddle by 3:00 p.m. He happened to meet John W. Smith, also headed for Gonzales. They rode along together, pausing for a last look at Bexar behind them. The sight was appalling. They could glimpse Mexican cavalry, lances gleaming, already occupying the town's Military Plaza.

A few minutes later, the two riders heard a cannon shot from the Alamo, meaning that its defenders were surrounded. Sutherland and Smith continued on, arriving in Gonzales on the afternoon of the 24th. Soon they were gathering small groups of men, alarmed by the news from Travis. Not only was there alarm, plans were being made to respond. Among the planners was George Kimball, owner of a small but prospering hat shop in Gonzales.

Bonham, riding back to Bexar from Gonzales, also heard the cannon's BOOM! It signaled the bad news that the Alamo was surrounded. As he paused, a man riding from Bexar reined-up. It was a courier named John Johnson, bearing another appeal for Fannin's help for the Alamo.

On February 23, Travis and Bowie had jointly written another letter to Fannin:

"We have removed all our men into the Alamo, where we will make such resistance as is due to our honour, and that of the country, until we can get assistance from you, *which we expect you to forward immediately.* (italics added) In this extremity, we hope you will send us all the men you can spare promptly. We have one hundred and forty-six men, who are determined never to retreat. We have but little provisions, but enough to serve us till you and your men arrive. *We deem it unnecessary to repeat to a brave officer, who knows his duty, that we call on him for assistance."* (italics added)

On February 24, Travis had penned his heroic "Victory or Death" declaration—not only to Texans but to "all Americans." The initial messenger of Travis' words was Captain Albert Martin, from Gonzales, thirty miles distant. Martin, age 30, knew the back roads well, even in the dark, as he spurred his mount out the Alamo main gate.

The next day Martin reached Gonzales and passed Travis' words on to a second, even younger, messenger named Launcelot Smithers. Despite Martin's haste, he had managed to scribble on the back of Travis's message his own postscript: "Hurry all the men you can."

Smithers galloped off toward San Felipe, another ninety miles away. A blast of icy weather from the north encouraged him to an even faster pace and he reached San Felipe early on Saturday, February 27. Citizens of San Felipe gathered at 11:00 to argue about a common resolution of support.

Smithers had added his own note to that of Captain Martin on the back of the Travis letter, which should have made the citizens' discussion even easier.

Smithers' hastily-scrawled resolution was simple:

"I hope that Everyone will Randeves at Gonzales as soon as posebe as the Brave Soldiers are suffering. Do not neglect the powder. is very scarce and should not be delad one moment."

Quicker than thought possible, George Kimball, John Flanders and Dolphin Floyd formed a group which became a home guard unit, initially of 22 men. They voted Kimball their lieutenant and gave themselves the grand title of "The Gonzales Ranging Company of Mounted Volunteers."

Others signed up, among them the same Captain Albert

Martin who had delivered Travis' "Victory or Death" letter on February 25. Martin was eager to return to the Alamo.

By Saturday, February 27, the Gonzales Ranging Company had assembled with weapons, ammunition, bedrolls and a few rations. Twenty-eight men rode out of Gonzales, picking up more volunteers on the way. They soon numbered 32 men.

They rested during the day (February 29) and crossed the San Antonio River at sunset. Nearing the Alamo after midnight they were challenged by a voice speaking English:

"Do you wish to go into the fort, gentlemen?" The question came from a dark horseman just ahead, apparently observing their progress.

One tired voice from the Gonzales group was quick to answer "Yes!"

At this, the unknown horseman swung into their lead until John W. Smith voiced his suspicions about this strange man.

Smith called out, "Boys, it's time to be after shooting that fellow!"

The unknown horseman spurred his horse and disappeared into the dark before anyone could react. Whether the horseman was friend or foe, no one ever knew.

Quietly, the 32 Gonzales men continued through the brush but with more caution until they eventually saw before them the walls of the Alamo.

It was not a warm welcome. A shot rang out from the fort and one of the men of the Ranging Company was wounded in the foot. His oaths and accent convinced the Alamo defenders that here was another Texan—or Texans—wanting inside. A lantern was lit, the postern gate opened a crack and 28 of the 32 volunteers from Gonzales were joyously welcomed into the Alamo at 3:00 a.m., March 1.

The defenders were as jubilant—if not more so—than when they received Colonel Crockett and his Tennessee sharpshooters. This was positively the greatest event since the siege began. An impromptu concert of bagpipe and fiddle by Crockett and John MacGregor began while Travis gave permission to fire two rounds from a 12-pounder at a house on the Main Plaza suspected of being Santa Ana's headquarters. The target was hit. Unfortunately, the latter was not at home, perhaps, at the time, being "wed" to the unsuspecting beautiful *senorita.*

Travis was less than jubilant, despite the music provided by Crockett's fiddle and McGregor's bagpipes. Rations were short…and getting shorter. The Gonzales volunteers had failed to bring extra food or ammunition.

Usually there were only two meals a day, both of beef, provided the garrison. Sanitation within the old mission was poor and health problems multiplied, as evinced by the growing sick calls seen by Doctor Amos Pollard at his small hospital in the "long" barracks. Dysentery, diarrhea and fever were endemic.

Originally, the Gonzales volunteers numbered 32 men but four were unable to evade the Mexican patrols. One of the four, Sam Bastian, explained:

"When near the fort we were discovered and fired upon by Mexican troops. Most of the party got through; but I and three others had to take to the chaparral to save our lives."

Due to the scouting abilities of Colonel Crockett, his party discovered a large group of volunteers sheltering near Cibolo Creek. He led them through the Mexican positions after midnight on March 4, causing another celebration.

# SEVEN

## MORE APPEALS, EVEN LESS RESULTS

IF HE WAS discouraged by the burgeoning shortages of men, provisions, ammunition, medical supplies and sanitation, it wasn't evident in Travis' eagerness to write and dispatch more appeals for assistance. On February 25, he appealed directly to Major General Sam Houston, commander of the Texas army. If other appeals had been ignored, certainly the Commander-in-Chief would take immediate remedial action.

In his report, Travis detailed Santa Ana's positions around the Alamo, to include estimated strengths and disposition of artillery, cavalry and reserves. Concluding with terms as powerful as those he used in the "Victory or Death" proclamation, Travis wrote:

"Do hasten on aid to me as rapidly as possible, as from the superior number of the enemy, it will be impossible for us to keep them out much longer. If they overpower us, we fall a sacrifice at the shrine of our country, and we hope posterity and our country will do our memory justice. Give me help, oh my Country!"

Since this message to Houston was so vital and compelling, it should be delivered by a messenger capable of answering the General's anticipated questions.

Travis put the question of who the messenger should be to a council of officers called for this purpose. After considerable discussion, the council selected Captain Juan Seguin.

Travis demurred, arguing that Seguin's services were more needed in the Alamo, not out delivering another appeal.

The council won; Travis conceded.

First, Captain Seguin needed a good horse, his own being lame. He ran to his friend Jim Bowie's sickroom. Bowie, bedridden and weak, agreed to loan his horse. Seguin and his orderly, Antonio Cruz, rode into the dark, rainy night, heading for Gonzales where Houston was presumed to be marshalling more troops.

The two friends, Juan Seguin and Jim Bowie, never were to see each other again.

Seguin and Cruz soon encountered a Mexican outpost and slowly approached it, pretending to be fellow Mexican compatriots. Almost at the outpost barrier, Seguin and Cruz suddenly spurred their mounts and barely escaped the shots fired after them.

They managed to make their way safely through the Mexican positions encircling the Alamo. After riding all night and escaping Mexican patrols, they met a Captain DeSauque, from Fannin's command, at Cibolo Creek. The captain told them that Fannin was already on the march to relieve the Alamo and would be there in two days.

Seguin, awaiting Fannin at the creek, thought it best to send Travis' communication via messenger to Fannin anyway. Fannin's eventual reply was extremely disappointing: he had about-faced and returned his "relief" column to Goliad.

Travis sat at his desk on the bitter, windy night of February 27, working on another appeal to Fannin for help. He handed the message to the man he perhaps trusted most, his friend, relative and fellow-South Carolinian, Jim Bonham.

Bonham had been successful in making his way through

the Mexican lines once before and Travis hoped he could repeat that dangerous feat. Bonham assured Travis that he would return, "God willing." This time he tied a white handkerchief around his hat to identify him to the Alamo sentinels when he eventually returned on the run.

Alone, Bonham galloped at full speed through the partially-open northern postern gate and into the dark night. On February 29, he arrived at Fannin's office in Fort Defiance/Goliad/LaBahia to find the latter moodily staring at his muddy boots. Fannin had returned from his abortive overnight attempt to march a relief column to the Alamo. He gave scant attention to Bonham's report and request to again go to the aid of the beleaguered Alamo garrison. "No," was his quick answer to the young lieutenant.

Paternally, Fannin added, "You'd better stay here with us instead of trying to get through those Mexican lines again. Stay here."

Bonham's decision was as quick as Fannin's

"No. I promised to get help. I'll try elsewhere." With that, he remounted his jaded horse and headed again to Gonzales.

Reaching there late on March 1, Bonham found mostly women and children, George Kimball and his "Gonzales 32" had already departed for the Alamo.

Surprisingly, Bonham found there a previous messenger from the Alamo, young Ben Highsmith. Highsmith had left the Alamo with an appeal for help even before Santa Ana completely surrounded Bexar. His appeal denied, Highsmith found his return to the Alamo blocked by Mexican troops near Powder House Hill. They chased him all the way back to Gonzales.

For a second time in a matter of hours, Bonham reiterated his steadfastness:

"I will report the result of my mission to Travis or die in the attempt."

He tightened the cinch on his horse, climbed up and set out for the Alamo early the next morning, March 2. About 11:00 a.m., March 3, Bonham succeeded in riding through the gates of the Alamo, white handkerchief fluttering on his hat, with the demoralizing news that Fannin and his "relief column" were not coming. Bonham was the last Texan to enter the surrounded Alamo.

Disappointed—but as steadfast as Lieutenant Bonham—Colonel Travis penned another report, this one to the President of the Texas Convention meeting at Washington on-the-Brazos. The report was another Travis summation of the Alamo's situation, the high morale of his men defending this "great and decisive ground" plus what they needed to continue fighting.

Travis was plainly disappointed in Colonel Fannin when he wrote to the Texas Convention's President the following:

> "…Col. Fannin is said to be on the march to this place with reinforcements; *but I fear it is not true.* (italics added) As I have repeatedly sent to him for aid without receiving any. Col. Bonham, my special messenger, arrived at Labahia fourteen days ago, with a request for aid; and the arrival of the enemy in Bexar ten days ago. I sent an express to Col. F. which arrived in Goliad the next day, urging him to send us reinforcements (none have arrived).
>
> "I look to the colonies alone for aid; unless it arrives soon, I shall have to fight the enemy on his own terms. I will do the best I can under the circumstances, and I feel confident that the determined valor and desperate courage, heretofore evinced by my men, will not fail them in the last struggle, and although they

> may be sacrificed to the vengeance of a Gothic
> enemy, the victory will cost the enemy so
> dear that it will be worse for him than defeat.
> I hope your honorable body will hasten
> reinforcements. Our supply of ammunition is
> limited. God and Texas. Victory or death."

As to their needs, Travis was very specific: "at least 500 pounds of cannon powder, 200 rounds of six, nine, twelve and eighteen-pound balls and ten kegs of rifle powder…"

A different tone entirely was used in Travis' letter to his friend, Jesse Grimes, a Delegate at the Convention:

"I am still here in fine spirits and well to do…." Then later, he turned to the subject of independence, the reason for the efforts of his hungry, poorly-equipped men encircled by a much stronger, massacre-minded enemy:

"Let the Convention go on and make a declaration of independence, and we will then understand, and the world will understand, what we are fighting for. If independence is not declared, I shall lay down my arms, and so will the men under my command. but under the flag of independence we are ready to peril our lives a hundred times a day and to drive away the monster (italics added) who is fighting us under a blood-red flag, threatening to murder all prisoners and make Texas a waste desert…If my countrymen do not rally to my relief, I am determined to perish in defense of this place, and my bones shall reproach my country for her neglect."

Realizing that this might be his last message out of the Alamo before the Mexicans' final assault, Travis also wrote a note to David Ayers who was caring for Travis' infant son, Charles, in San Felipe:

"Take care of my little boy. If the country should be saved, I may make him a splendid fortune; but if the country should be lost and I should perish, he will have nothing but the proud recollection that he is the son of a man who died for his country."

Others of the Alamo's soldiers had the same sober thought about last messages. Many men wrote brief notes to family members whom they might never see again. The volunteer who would carry their messages out of the Alamo was John W. Smith, the garrison's best carpenter, nicknamed "El Colorado" because of his red beard.

He stood in the plaza late on March 3, tending his horse when not stuffing last letters and notes into his saddlebags.

Colonel Travis planned a diversion at the northern postern, to cover Smith's exit through the main gate. A group of Bowie's volunteers would slip outside, quietly work their way toward the sugar mill, then begin firing at Mexican positions and scamper back inside. At the same time, Smith would ride hell-for-leather out the main gate and into the darkness to Washington-on-the-Brazos.

Travis handed Smith his messages, then remembered to tell him that the 18-pounder would be fired three times a day to announce that the Alamo was intact and had not fallen. In farewell, Travis slapped the horse sharply on its hindquarters and Smith was on his way.

A feeling that something was about to happen hung in the garrison for several more days. Mexican artillery fire was incessant and few defenders were able to sleep more than an hour or two. Consequently, the defenders were all exhausted. Beyond the walls, even the Mexicans appeared to be quiet in the early hours of March 6.

The quiet even affected the usually high-spirited Colonel Crockett, who dourly commented, "I think we had better march out and die in the open air. I don't like to be hemmed up."

It was then that Travis decided to dispatch yet another courier/messenger, urging Fannin to quickly send reinforcements, ammunition and provisions. His message was the same: join us! By now, experienced, trusted messengers with good horses, who could ride like the wind, were scarce.

Travis selected a sixteen-year old boy known for his superb horsemanship to carry yet another message to Fannin . The messenger was James L. Allen, riding bareback out the postern, into the darkness with a last plea to Fannin.

Not only did the young bareback rider evade the Mexicans, who were quietly assembling to make the final assault on the Alamo, he made it all the way to Goliad unscathed. There, Allen commented upon the destruction that the Mexican artillery was having on the Alamo's old walls and fortifications.

Captain John S. Brooks at Goliad relayed Allen's message and observations to Fannin with the sad observation:

"It is feared that Bexar will be taken, and that the devoted courage of the brave defenders will be of no avail."

If Fannin replied, it was neither recorded nor remembered.

# EIGHT

## EERIE QUIET

LIEUTENANT BONHAM COMPLETED his mission assigned him by Colonel Travis and returned safely to the Alamo, not once but twice. After making his disappointing reports about Fannin's dithering, Bonham climbed to the cannon positions which Captain Dickinson commanded, atop the chapel.

Along with his companions, Bonham serviced, aimed and fired the three 12-pounders on the roof. The duty was not easy: digging more ditches and building earthen parapets below plus cleaning and firing the cannon above, all called for better rations than dried beef and tasteless coffee. There was little rest manning the cannon during daylight, even less once darkness fell, due to the incessant Mexican artillery rounds falling inside the compound.

The weather turned bitterly cold yet there was little wood for fires.

Ammunition was scarce. The cannon serviced by Bonham and others could not return all the Mexican artillery fire because of their lack of powder and ball.

Travis praised Crockett's performance throughout the long siege. "He proved to be as steady under fire as he was spinning yarns or playing a jig on his violin. He animated men to do their duty." Travis also often sought Crockett's advice and opinion.

Enrique, son of slain Alamo defender Gregorio Esparza, remembered Crockett years later as the leading spirit:

"He was everywhere. He went to every exposed point and personally directed the fighting. Travis was chief in command but he depended more on the judgment of Crockett and that brave man's integrity than his own. Bowie, too, was brave and dauntless, but he was ill. Prone upon his cot, he was unable to see much that was going on about him and the others were too engrossed to stop and tell him."

An exception was Crockett, who often visited Bowie's sickroom in the "low" barracks. At one such visit, Davy cleaned and loaded Bowie's pistols and rifle and placed them within reach of his cot.

To take Bowie's mind off his failing condition, Crockett asked him about the famous sandbar fight which gained Bowie and his famous fighting knife (designed by Jim's brother, Rezin) their fearful reputations. The fight occurred on a river sandbar near Natchez, Mississippi, in September, 1827, Jim admitted in a low voice. Eventually, he related the results of the fight: two men killed and two badly wounded, Bowie among them. He was shot four times and badly cut five.

His opponent, a Norris Wright, rushed at the wounded Bowie with a cane sword. Jim struck at Wright with his big knife "twisting it to cut his heart strings," and the fight was over.

On his cot, Bowie coughed with the effort of re-telling the incident. Once settled again in the blanket, he recounted another, less-known fight with Indians in Texas.

Bowie, his brother Rezin, seven other Americans and two servants were surrounded by an estimated 160 Caddo, Waco and Tawakoni warriors. During the 13 hour siege that followed, 40 Indians were killed and 30 wounded. Jim's companions suffered one killed and three wounded.

Bowie's exertions at telling the stories made him groggy and he excused himself with "Gotta sleep now."

The garrison immediately noticed the unusual quiet when the Mexican cannon became silent. The sudden quiet was foreboding.

Suspicious of the eerie quiet, Crockett asked for the laundered clothing some of the ladies had washed for him. He announced, "I'm going to be killed tomorrow. I aim to go in clean clothing so I can get a proper burial." No one was certain if he was joking or not.

Many of the men took him seriously. They gave the women their personal possessions, like watches and jewelry, to hide away.

No help was in sight. Food and munitions were so low that Travis pleaded not only for help. He said that every new man must bring additional food and ammunition.

General Filisola later wrote that Travis unsuccessfully attempted to propose surrender to Santa Ana if the lives of all his men were guaranteed. Santa Ana's curt reply was that Travis must surrender unconditionally without any guarantees—including the lives of Travis and his men—because there were no guarantees for "traitors."

At this point Travis may have assembled the entire garrison "in a single line" in the Plaza. The lone surviving Alamo defender, Private Louis Rose, supposedly memorized portions of Travis' last speech to his men:

"Within a few days—perhaps in a very few hours—we must all be in eternity. This is our destiny and we cannot avoid it. This is our certain doom.

"I have deceived you long by the promise of help. But I crave your pardon. In deceiving you, I also deceived myself, having first being deceived by others."

He then explained how Fannin and the Convention had failed them in providing the reinforcements and support requested and so desperately needed.

According to the recollections of the illiterate Private Louis Rose, Travis then asked if the men preferred to surrender or to escape. He answered his own question by urging that they not only stay, but kill as many of the enemy as possible.

Anyone wishing to escape, he continued—according to Rose—was free to leave. Travis then took his sword and walked the length of the single rank of men as he scratched a line in the sand with the blade.

All who would stay with him and fight should step over the line in the sand and join him.

Louis Rose even remembered the name of the first man to step over the line to join Travis. It was twenty-six year old Tapley Holland, a Private in Captain Carey's artillery battery. Originally from Ohio, Holland now lived in nearby Grimes County, Texas.

Every man except one—even the sick and wounded—stepped over the line to join Travis. Even Bowie, on his cot (which had been carried down to the Plaza) was adamant about crossing that line in the sand.

"Boys," Bowie spoke up as loudly as he could. "I am not able to come to you, but I wish some of you would be so kind as to remove my cot over there."

Crockett and three others picked up Bowie and cot and moved him over the line.

Only Rose remained on the other side of the line in the sand.

Bowie, a friend, looked at Rose and said, "You seem to be unwilling to die with us."

Rose nodded, later shouldered his pack, crawled over a wall and dropped from sight.

He evaded Mexican lancers in the nearby brush and

Roy Sullivan

mesquite, eventually making his way to Grimes County where a local family cared for his terribly mesquite-scratched arms and legs.

Often called to defend his desertion, Rose said simply "I wasn't ready to die." Die he did, but much later in 1850. Rose was buried in an unmarked grave near Logansport, Louisiana.

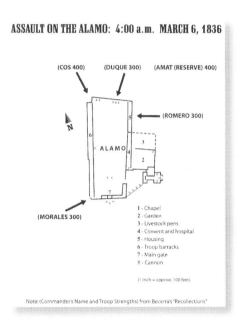

Credits: N.K. Rogers photograph (at the bottom)

# NINE

## THE MEXICANS LAY SIEGE AND PLAN ASSAULT

NOTE: THE FOLLOWING are excerpts from the journal of Mexican Colonel Juan N. Almonte, aide-de-camp of General Santa Ana, published in the *New York Herald* in June, 1836. Almonte's journal offers observations about the weather, Santa Ana's personal reconnaissances, general officers' consensus concerning artillery support and when to attack, plus Santa Ana's decision on the method and time of attack. These activities lead to the final, March 6 assault upon the Alamo and its beleaguered, doomed defenders.

"February 24: Very early this morning a new (artillery) battery was commenced on the bank of the river, about 350 yards from the Alamo. It was finished in the afternoon, and a brisk fire was kept up from it until the 18-pounder and another piece [on the walls] was dismounted. The President reconnoitered on horseback, passing within musket shot of the fort. According to a spy, four of the enemy were killed. At evening the music struck up, and went [on] to entertain the enemy with it and some grenades. In the night, according to the statement of a spy, some 30 men arrived at the fort from Gonzales.

"February 25: The firing from our batteries was commenced early. The General-in-Chief with the battalion de Cazadores, crossed the river and posted themselves at the Alamo—that is to say, in the houses near the fort. A new fortification was commenced by us near the house of McMullen. In the random firing the enemy wounded 4 of the Cazadores de Matamoros battalion, and 2 of the battalion of Jimenes, and killed one corporal and a soldier of the battalion of Matamoros. Our fire ceased in the afternoon. In the night two batteries were erected by us on the other side of the river in the Alameda of the Alamo—the battalion of Matamoros was also posted there, and the cavalry was posted on the hills to the east of the enemy, and in the road from Gonzales at the Casa Mata Antigua. At half past eleven at night we retired. The enemy in the night, burnt the straw and wooden houses in their vicinity, but did not attempt to set fire with their guns to those in our rear. A strong north wind commenced at nine at night.

"February 26: The northern wind continued very strong; the thermometer fell to 39 degrees, and during the day remained at 60 degrees. At daylight there was a slight skirmish between the enemy and a small party of the division of the east, under the command of General Sesma. During the day the firing from our cannon was continued. The enemy did not reply, except now and then. At night the enemy burnt the small houses near the parapet of the battalion of San Luis, on the other side of the river. Some sentinels were advanced. In the course of the day the enemy sallied out for wood and water, and were opposed by our marksmen. The north wind continues.

"February 27: The northern wind was strong at daybreak, and continued all the night.

Thermostat at 39 degrees. Lieutenant Manuel Menchaco [Menchaca of the Bexar Presidial Company] was sent with a party of men for corn, cattle and hogs at the Ranchos (small farms) of Seguin and Flores. It was determined to cut off the water from the enemy on the side next to the old mill. There was little firing from either side during the day. The enemy worked hard to repair some entrenchments. In the afternoon the President was observed by the enemy and fired at. In the night a courier extraordinary was dispatched to the city of Mexico, informing the Government of the taking of Bexar and also to Gen'ls Urrea, Filisola, Cos and Vital Fernandez. No private letters were sent.

"February 28: The weather abated somewhat. Thermostat at 40 degrees at 7A.M. News were received that a reinforcement to the enemy was coming by road from La Bahia, in number 200. It was not true. The cannonading continued.

"February 29: The weather changed—thermostat at 5 degrees, in the night it commenced blowing hard from the west. In the afternoon the battalion of Allende took post at the east of the Alamo. The President reconnoitered. One of our soldiers was killed in the night. The wind changed to the north at midnight. About that time Gen. Sesma left the camp with the cavalry of Dolores and the infantry of Allende to meet the enemy coming from La Bahia or Goliad to the aid of the Alamo. Gen. Castrillon on guard.

"March 1: The wind subsided, but the weather continued cold—thermometer at 6 degrees in the morning—day clear. Early in the morning Gen. Sesma wrote from the Mission de la Espada that there was no such enemy, and that he had reconnoitered as far as Tinaja, without finding any traces of them. The cavalry returned to camp, and the infantry to this city. At 12 o'clock the President went out to reconnoiter the mill site to the northwest of the Alamo. Lieut. Col. Ampudia was commissioned to construct more trenches. In the afternoon the enemy fired two 12 pound shots at the house of the President, one of which struck the house, and the other passed over it. Nothing more of consequence occurred. Night cold— Thermometer 34 degrees Fahrenheit, and 1 degree Reamur.

"March 2: Commenced clear and pleasant—thermometer 34 degrees—no wind. An Aid of Col. Duque arrived with dispatches from Arroyo Hondo, dated 1s inst.; in reply, he was ordered to leave the river Medina, and arrive the next day at 12 or 1 o'clock. Gen. J. Ramirez came to breakfast with the President. Information was received that there was corn at the farm of Seguin, and Lieut. Menchaca was sent with a party for it. The President discovered, in the afternoon, a covered road within pistol shot of the Alamo, and posted the battalion of Jimenes there. At 5 A.M. Bringas went out to meet Ganoa.

"March 3: Commenced clear at 40 degrees, without wind. The enemy fired a few cannon and musket shots at the city. I wrote to Mexico and my sister, directed them to send their letters to Bexar, and that before 3 months the campaign would be ended. The General-in-Chief went out to reconnoiter. A battery was erected on the north of the Alamo within musket shot. Official dispatches were received from Gen. Urrea, announcing that he had routed the colonists at San Patricio—killing sixteen and taking 21 prisoners. The bells were rung. The battalion of Zapadores, Adama and Toluca arrived. The enemy attempted a sally in the night at the Sugar Mill, but were repulsed by our advance.

"March 4: The day commenced windy, but not cold—thermostat 42 degrees. Commenced firing very early, which the enemy did not return. In the afternoon one or two shots were fired by them. A meeting of General and Colonels was held, at which Generals Cos, Sesma, and Castrillon were present. (Generals Amador and Venura Mora did not attend—the former having been suspended, and the latter in active commission.) Also present, Colonels Francisco Duque, battalion of Toluca—Orisnuela, battalion of Aldama—Romero, battalion of Matamoros—Amat, battalion of Zapadores, and the Major of battalion of San Luis did not attend, being engaged in actual commission. I was also called. After a long conference, Cos, Castrillon, Orisnuela, and Romero were of the opinion that the Alamo should be assaulted—first opening a breach with the two cannon and the two mortars, and that they should wait the arrival of the two 12 pounders expected on Monday the 7th. The President, Gen. Ramirez, and I were of the opinion that the 12 pounders should not be waited for, but that the assault made. Colonels Duque and Amat and the Major of the San Luis battalion did not give any definite opinion about either of the two modes of assault proposed. In this state of things remained—the General not making any definite resolution. In the night the north parapet was advanced toward the enemy through the water course. A Lieutenant of Engineers conducted the entrenchment. A messenger was dispatched to Urrea.

"March 5: The day commenced very moderate—thermometer 50 degrees—weather clear. A brisk fire was commenced from our north battery against the enemy, which was not answered, except now and then. At mid-day the thermometer rose to 68 degrees. The President determined to make the assault and it was agreed that the four columns of attack were to be commanded by Generals Cos, Duque, Romero and Morales, and second in command, Generals Castrillon, Amador and Minon. For this purpose, the points of attack were examined by the commanding officers, and they came to the conclusion that they should muster at 12 o'clock tonight, and at 4 o'clock tomorrow morning (Sunday, 6th) the attack should be made."

Santa Ana gave specific orders to his staff about the morning of March 6. He was to be awakened at 3:00 a.m., well ahead of his usual time of 9:30. After coffee and two freshly-baked croissants and guava jelly, he would don his field uniform, minus decorations. The guard companies would escort him to the forward observation post he had selected near the south artillery position where he could observe and direct the assault against the enemy fortifications.

# TEN

## THE QUIET IS SHATTERED

THE EARLY MORNING hours of March 6 were chilly, if not downright cold. Stubborn remnants of fog swathed the battered walls of the Alamo. Inside, exhausted defenders dozed beside their muskets, rifles and cannon.

But outside—if anyone listened carefully—there were muted but increasing sounds of an army moving to contact at 4 a.m.

The Alamo's officer of the day was Captain John J. Baugh, formerly of Virginia. He was the first person inside the fort to hear the bugle sounds and distant yells of "Viva Mejico! Viva Santa Ana!"

Captain Baugh began hollering as loudly as he could. "The Mexicans are coming! The Mexican are coming!" He rushed into Travis' room on the west wall where Travis and Jim slept.

As the Mexicans rushed to their assigned assault positions on the perimeters of the Alamo, Santa Ana's band began playing the Deguello, the old tune reminding the Mexican troops to show no mercy.

Travis awoke with a start, grabbed his sword and shotgun and rushed to the cannon emplacement on the northeast corner of the north wall called the Fortin de Teran. Jim followed Travis closely, brandishing his own weapon.

Capturing the north wall where Travis stood was the

immediate objective of Mexican Colonel Francisco Duque's column of 300 soldados.

"Come on, boys!" Travis encouraged his few troops on the wall. "The Mexicans are upon us and we'll give them hell!"

A frenzy of shouting from Duque's column attacking the wall aided the Texans manning the cannon on the Fortin de Teran to locate their first massed target. A single blast from the hastily–aimed cannon killed dozens of attackers from the Toluca Battalion.

Colonel Duque's aide, De la Pena, grimaced at the bloody result. He wrote "The officers were unable to repress this act of folly (the soldiers' loud cheering) which was paid for dearly."

Another blast from the Texas cannon fatally wounded and immobilized Colonel Duque as well as many others. During the rush at the north wall, his own men trampled Duque underfoot. Immediately, General Manuel Castrillon was ordered to replace the fallen Duque.

The Texas cannon on the northwest corner of the north wall also began firing, at the massed attackers. This time some 40 men of the Aldama Battalion of General Martin Perfecto de Cos' column fell dead or mortally wounded.

Colonel Travis leaned over the wall and fired his shotgun into the mass of screaming soldiers attempting to scale the north wall on clumsy homemade ladders. The Mexicans fired back, hitting Travis in the forehead. He fell backward, face-up, on the parapet. Seeing his boss dead or dying, Jim retreated and took cover in a nearby west wall room, firing his weapon several times at the Mexicans coming over the wall.

Looking out a loophole in the wall of his hideaway, Jim saw a Mexican officer (whom he later identified as General Mora) crouching on the parapet near Travis. The Texan now was trying to sit up with the aid of his sword.

Mora swung his own sword at Travis, trying to decapitate

him, Jim thought. With his last strength, Travis parried the blow and sank his own sword into Moras' body.

Both died on the parapet.

Travis, the Alamo's commander, was probably the first Texan to die during the Mexican final assault on the old mission.

On the east wall, Colonel Jose Maria Romero's 300 troops were also being decimated by grapeshot being fired from a cannon mounted on the top of the chapel. The left portion of Romero's column was torn apart by the fire. The right side, seeing their comrades being badly bloodied, turned away to avoid the same fate.

Safely watching the slaughter on the north wall from an earthworks observation post to the northwest, Santa Ana decided it was time to commit his reserves.

This was another 300 soldiers under the command of Colonel Augustin Amat. This commitment was intended to re-energize the stalled attack on the north wall where the commands of both Cos and Castrillon were panicking.

Watching his reserve fare no better against Texas marksmanship than the others, Santa Ana even ordered his general staff into the fray.

Lieutenant De la Pena wrote "the gallant reserve merely added to the noise and the victims…there was no necessity for them to engage in combat."

The reserves fired their weapons while running toward the wall. Most of their rounds

ricocheted off the wall or struck the troops ahead of them.

General Filisola, next in command to Santa Ana, later estimated three quarters of the Mexican casualties resulted from friendly fire. "Not a fourth of them were the result of enemy fire," he maintained.

Lieutenant De la Pena sadly observed the confusion at the north wall:

"A quarter of an hour had elapsed during which our soldiers remained in a terrible situation, wearing themselves out as they climbed in quest of a less obscure death than that visited upon them, crowded in a single mass."

An estimated three or four hundred bodies lay heaped in a large half-circle radiating from the bottom of the north wall.

De la Pena also decried the Mexican casualties incurred during the later door-to-door fighting along the 'long" barracks:

"The tumult was great, the disorder frightful; it seemed as if the furies had descended upon us; different groups of soldiers were firing in all directions, on their comrades and on their officers, so that one was as likely to die by a friendly hand as by an enemy's."

Colonel Morales' column, charged with taking the main gate and the palisaded area defended by Crockett's Tennessee sharpshooters, initially fared badly. The fire power from Davy's "boys" stalled the Morales advance. Morales ordered a retreat to the southwest of the Alamo. It was a mistake because his troops were then vulnerable to the fire of the 18-pounder mounted on the southwest corner. Partially shielded by a group of wooden shacks or jacales, Morales revised his attack plan: first eliminate that 18-pounder and crew on the roof, then wipe out the palisade defenders, lastly storm the chapel door and kill the Texans inside.

Surrounded and greatly outnumbered, Colonel Crockett and his Tennesseans probably ran out of ammunition nor had the time to reload their single shot muskets. Instead, they relied on pistols, knives and musket butts.

Not one of Crockett's small group of thirteen survived the Mexican onslaught in their palisaded area between the southwest corner of the chapel and the southeast wall of the "low" barracks.

Earlier, they may have rushed from their fenced position to lend fire support to the defenders of the west wall. Crockett and crew were forced backwards, deeper into the position assigned by Travis and were eventually overwhelmed and slaughtered by Morales' troops.

Famous historian Walter Lord wrote:

"Crockett's Tennesseans, at bay near the palisade, battled with a wild fury that awed even the attackers. Individual names and deeds were lost forever in the seething mass of knives, pistols, fists and broken gun stocks…"

A second, more concentrated attack by Morales carried the day and the big cannon on the southwest corner eliminated. Captain Dickinson and all his crew, including Lieutenant Bonham, were dead.

Finally, on the north wall, General Castrillon's column gained a foothold and the Mexicans poured over the top of the wall "like sheep."

Mexican Sergeant Francisco Becerra later described the assault in his book, A Mexican Sergeant's Recollection of the Alamo and San Jacinto. Although criticized by some as being the least reliable Alamo eye-witness, particularly about the death of Colonel Crockett, his descriptions of the March 6 assault are detailed and useful.

"Our troops, inspired by success, continued the attack with energy and boldness. The Texians (note: former spelling of Texans) fought like devils. It was short range—muzzle to muzzle—hand to hand—musket and rifle—bayonet and Bowie knife—all were mingled in confusion. Here a squad of Mexicans, there a Texian or two. The crash of firearms, the shouts of defiance, the cries of the dying and wounded, made a din almost infernal. The Texians defended desperately each inch of the fort, overpowered by numbers, they would be forced to abandon a room. They would rally in the next, and defend it until further resistance became impossible.

"Gen. Eugenio Tolza's command (the fourth column led by Colonel Morales) forced an entrance at the door of the church building. He met the same determined resistance without and within. He won by force of numbers and at a great cost of life."

Mexican troops crossing the plaza from the north wall met Texan fire from the cluster of rooms along the west and east walls. Usually more fatally, they were fired upon by the Morales column on the south side.

General Cos ordered a bugler to sound "cease fire," in order to reduce the wild, indiscriminate firing by his troops. Many were in a killing frenzy and either did not hear or obey the bugle call. The firing continued well after the last Alamo defender was killed. De la Pena estimated that 50,000 rounds were fired in a little less than one hour. If his estimate was correct, the ammunition supply of the entire Mexican army must have been seriously depleted that day, March 6, 1836.

A few defenders, among them Alamo quartermaster Eliel Melton, seeing no chance of survival, attempted to escape over a wall and into a ditch. The number of Texans following his example is unknown. Once outside the wall, they were easy prey for General Sesma's mounted lancers waiting on the other side of the wall.

By 9:00 that morning, the sun not yet up but the battle was over. Susannah Dickinson, wife of Captain Dickinson, the artillery commander, recalled Crockett somehow found her room earlier. Crockett, she said, fell to his knees said a short prayer, then walked out to rejoin the battle.

During the height of the battle, Captain Dickinson rushed into the baptistery where his wife hid, exclaiming " Great God, Sue! The Mexicans are inside our walls! All is lost! If they spare you, save my child!"

With that the Captain kissed his wife, then returned to Lieutenant Bonham and crew, busily firing the cannon on the chapel roof.

Dickinson was one of the famous "Old Eighteen" residents of Gonzalez who earlier defeated Mexicans sent to retrieve an old cannon used for Indian defense. Those eighteen men fired the first shot of the Texas revolution, under a homemade flag of a cannon barrel and proclamation "Come and Take It."

Elsewhere, throughout the Alamo plaza, Mexican soldiers who'd missed or neglected using their weapons on live Texans, instead used them on dead ones. Some of the soldados even reloaded their rifles and repeatedly fired into corpses.

In the plaza, adjoining rooms, the chapel and hospital, Mexican soldiers rushed among the wounded and ailing, killing everyone in their beds or cots. A new sport developed in the frenzy, using dead bodies for bayonet practice. Many bodies were mutilated, some decapitated, while the dead and dying were stripped of their clothing, shoes and personal possessions. Their officers failed to halt the atrocities and hysteria.

General Filisola later lamented, "There were deeds that we refrain from relating because of the sorrow that the account of the events would cause us."

General Santa Ana had no such scruples. He seemed unmoved as he walked among the piles of the dead and dying after the battle. Contemptuously, he compared the dead to "chickens."

"Much blood has been shed, but the battle is over," he remarked to Captain Fernando Urizza. "It was but a small affair." (italics added)

Sergeant Becerra of General Sesma's division wrote:

"Our loss in front of the Alamo was represented at two thousand killed, and more than three hundred wounded. The killed were generally struck on the head. The wounds were in the neck, or shoulder, seldom below that. The firing of the besieged was fearfully precise. When a Texas rifle was leveled on a Mexican, he was considered as good as dead. All this indicated the dual dauntless bravery and cool self-possession of the men who were engaged in a hopeless conflict with an enemy numbering more than twenty to one. They inflicted upon us a loss ten times greater than the loss they sustained.

"The victory of the Alamo was dearly bought. Indeed, the price in the end was well nigh the ruin of Mexico."

Even General-in-Chief Santa Ana briefly mentioned Texan courage in his autobiography: "…not one soldier showed signs of desiring to surrender, and with fierceness and valor, they died fighting."

Where was Santa Ana during the assault? In his book "Rendezvous at the Alamo," Virgil E. Baugh wrote:

"Castrillon, not Santa Ana, was the soul of the assault. The latter remained in his south battery, viewing the operations from the corner of a house which covered him, till he supposed the place was nearly mastered, when he moved up toward the Alamo, escorted by his aides and bands of music, but turned back on being greeted by a few shots from the upper part of the chapel. He, however, entered the area towards the close of the scene, and directed some of the last details of the butchery."

Roy Sullivan

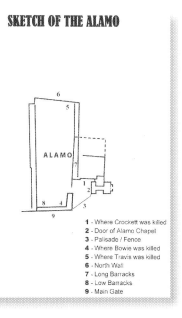

**SKETCH OF THE ALAMO**

ALAMO

1 - Where Crockett was killed
2 - Door of Alamo Chapel
3 - Palisade / Fence
4 - Where Bowie was killed
5 - Where Travis was killed
6 - North Wall
7 - Long Barracks
8 - Low Barracks
9 - Main Gate

*Where Crockett (1), Bowie (4) and Travis (5) Were Killed. Credit N.K. Rogers photograph*

# ELEVEN

## WHERE CROCKETT, BOWIE AND TRAVIS WERE KILLED

COLONEL TRAVIS, THE Alamo's commander, was likely the first Texan to die during the Mexican assault on March 6. Running to the north battery with Joe, his slave, he stood on the walls, exhorting his men. "Hurrah, my boys!"

Leaning over the wall, he fired his shotgun into the climbing soldados. The Mexicans fired back, hitting Travis in the forehead. Mortally wounded, he fell backward, face-up, on the parapet near the wall.

According to Joe, he saw a Mexican officer crouching near Travis who was attempting to sit up. The Mexican officer, whom Joe identified as General Mora, tried to finish Travis with his sword. Somehow their roles were reversed. Travis sank his own sword into Mora's body and they both died on that parapet.

Lieutenant James Butler Bonham with Captain Almeron Dickinson and ten crewmen serviced the 12-pound cannon on the back platform of the chapel. Gregorio Esparza fired a smaller cannon from the south window below. Robert Evans, the "Master of Ordnance," kept ammunition flowing upstairs from the powder magazine until the end.

In response to the devastating fire from atop the chapel, Colonel Morales ordered the crew of the Mexican 18-pound cannon to retaliate. The chapel was raked by fire from the heavy cannon. Soon Bonham, Dickinson and the entire crew on the platform were dead.

Gregorio Esparza's body was found slumped beside his cannon. Francisco, his brother, approached General Cos and requested he be allowed to bury Gregorio. Since Francisco had fought under General Cos at Bexar, his wish to bury his brother was granted. Gregorio was the only Alamo defender to be buried, not burned in a pyre.

The manner of Colonel James Bowie's death is more of a mystery. He was discovered on his sickbed cot in the "low" barracks, according to Mayor/Alcalde of Bexar Francisco A. Ruiz. Some accounts say Bowie shot two Mexicans with his pistols (which previously had been cleaned and loaded for him by Crockett). Another report was that blood from a head wound was evident on the wall beside Bowie's cot. Yet another, that his body had been repeatedly bayoneted and mutilated in his bed.

There were at least two known reactions to Bowie's gruesome death. Santa Ana initially said Bowie's bravery earned him burial rather than burning. Santa Ana later reneged and Bowie's corpse was burned with all the other defenders.

Back home in Kentucky Bowie's mother, on hearing of her 40-year old son's death, said she bet "No wounds were found on my son's back."

In the case of Colonel David (Davy) Crockett, Mrs. Susannah Dickinson, wife of the Artillery captain, reported seeing Crockett's dead body as she was being escorted outside the church after the battle:

"As we passed through the enclosed ground in front of the church, I saw heaps of dead and dying. The Texans on an average killed between eight and ten Mexicans each, 182 Texans and 1600 Mexicans were killed.

"I recognized Colonel Crockett lying dead and mutilated between the church and the two-story barrack building, and even remember seeing his peculiar cap lying by his side."

Mayor Ruiz, ordered by Santa Ana to point out the bodies of the colonels, reported the following:

"On the north battery of the fortress lay the lifeless body of Col. Travis on the gun carriage, shot only in the forehead. Toward the west, and in the small fort opposite the city, we found the body of Col. Crockett. Col. Bowie was found dead in his bed in one of the rooms of the south side." (note: the Ruiz description of Crockett's body in a "small fort opposite the city" [the 'city' is probably the nearby huts of La Villita] could mean the palisaded, fenced area outside the chapel door which Crocket and his "Tennessee Boys" defended)

Bill Groneman, a Texas historian famous for his extensive research on Crockett's death, concludes in one of his studies, Death of a Legend:

"I think there is enough evidence to place Crockett's body in the area in front of the Alamo church, to the exclusion of any other place."

A metal marker reading "Legend States That David Crockett (Born August 17, 1786) Sacrificed His Life Here In Defense Of The Alamo On March 6, 1836." is embedded near the chapel door. This marker is located just to the left of the chapel main door.

# TWELVE
## CASUALTIES ON BOTH SIDES

INHABITANTS OF SAN Antonio de Bexar boasted that the very first Mexican casualty during the siege fell to Crockett's rifle at a range of over 200 yards. They also bragged that another of Davy's long-range shots almost hit General-in-Chief Santa Ana.

Santa Ana claimed to have lost only 70 men killed in action and 300 wounded. Mrs. Dickinson wrote that there were 140 defenders in the Alamo, all of whom were killed. She estimated Santa Ana's losses as 1500 killed and wounded.

Colonel Juan Almonte's journal entry for March 6 showed Mexican casualties were 65 killed and 223 wounded. According to Almonte, Texas losses were 250. He also recorded the "instant death" dealt some Alamo survivors. Almonte's anger at being robbed by his own men far exceeded his concern about those defenders who were captured, then "put to the sword."

Concerning this incident, he wrote:

"At 5 A.M. the columns were posted at their respective stations and at half past 5 the attack or assault was made, and continued until 6 a.m. when the enemy attempted in vain to fly, (note: Almonte may be referring to several defenders who leaped over the walls, attempting to escape toward Gonzales with Quartermaster Eliel Melton, but were killed by Sesma's cavalry) but they were overtaken and put to the Sword and only five women, one Mexican soldier (prisoner) and a black slave escaped from instant death."

Almonte continued:

"On the part of the enemy the result was, 250 killed, and seventeen pieces of artillery —a flag, muskets and firearms taken. Our loss was 60 soldiers and 5 officers killed, and 198 soldiers and 25 officers wounded—2 of the latter General officers.

"The battalion of Toluca lost 98 men between the wounded and killed. I was robbed by our soldiers."(italics added)

Mayor Ruiz generally agreed with Mrs. Dickinson's estimate of Mexican losses. "Santa Ana's loss was estimated at 1600 men. These were the flower of his army."

Another estimate, that of General Filisola: "Thus, although the Alamo fell, this triumph cost the Mexican army more than seventy dead and three hundred wounded."

The actual number of Mexican casualties may never be known since many of the wounded later died. Santa Ana refused to bring medical personnel with his army to Texas.

De la Pena, a critic of his general, wrote:

"The plight of our wounded was quite grievous and one could hardly enter the places erroneously called hospitals without trembling with horror. The wailing of the wounded and their just complaints penetrated the innermost recesses of the heart; there was no one to extract a bullet, no one to perform an amputation, and many unfortunates died whom medical science could have saved."

Historian Walter Lord, author of several books on the Alamo's last days, wrote as follows about Mexican casualties:

"…nineteen sources give nineteen different answers—ranging from 65 killed and 223 wounded (Colonel Almonte) to 2000 killed and 300 wounded (Sergeant Becerra)…Best estimate seems to be about 600 killed and wounded."

Mexican General Juan Jose Andrade compiled the following Mexican casualties: Officers, killed 8, wounded 18. Troops, killed 52, wounded 223.

Regardless of the exact number of Mexican casualties, less than 200 Texas defenders inflicted a casualty rate of approximately thirty percent during their short battle with a vastly larger enemy force.

As to Texas losses at the Alamo, Walter Lord wrote the following:

"Figures range from 180 to Santa Ana's ludicrous 600. Best estimate seems to be 183. This is the final figure give by Ramon Caro, the Mexican general's secretary."

Wikipedia's "Battle of the Alamo" assesses the casualties as follows: Texans, 182-257 killed; Mexicans, 400-600 killed and wounded.

Bill Groneman's meticulous 1990 study, "Alamo Defenders," names 221 total personnel (military and noncombatants) in the Alamo at one time or another. Of these, he lists 188 as killed in action.

# THIRTEEN
## THE FINAL ATROCITY

MAYOR RUIZ WAS summoned by Santa Ana after the battle. Despite the bloody bodies of the dead and wounded, many of them Mexican, being piled like cordwood in the plaza, Santa Ana was not satisfied. He insisted on personally seeing the corpses of the Alamo leaders. Ruiz claimed he could positively identify Travis, Bowie and Crockett, so he was ordered to point out their bodies to the General-in-Chief.

After identifying these bodies, Ruiz received another order from Santa Ana. Here is Ruiz' after-action report about his grisly detail:

"Santa Ana, after all the Mexicans were taken out, ordered wood to be brought to burn the bodies of the Texans. He sent a company of dragoons with me to bring wood and dry branches from the neighboring forest.

"About 3 o'clock in the afternoon, they commenced laying the wood and dry branches, upon which a file of dead bodies was placed; more wood was piled on them, and another file brought, and in this manner they were all arranged in layers. Kindling wood was distributed through the pile, and about 5 o'clock in the evening, it was lighted."

Roy Sullivan

A teenager living in Bexar, Pablo Diaz, remembered:

"I saw an immense pillar of flame shoot up a short distance to the south and east of the Alamo and the dense smoke from it rise high in the clouds. (On the third day) I noticed that the air was tainted with the terrible odor of many corpses, and I saw thousands of vultures flying over me…Looking eastward I saw a large crowd gathered.

"Intuitively I went to the place. The crowd was gathered around the smoldering embers and ashes of the fire I had seen from the mission…I did not need to make inquiry. The story was told by the silent witnesses before me. Fragments of flesh, bones and charred wood and ashes revealed it in all its terrible truth. Grease that had exuded from the bodes saturated the earth for several feet beyond the ashes and smoldering mesquite faggots."

For several weeks a gray smoke haze marked the site of these atrocities. The haze and the circling birds of prey were visible for several miles distant from the town. Town people tied handkerchiefs about their noses for days.

Designated later to pay honor to the remains of the Alamo defenders was Lieutenant Colonel Juan Seguin. His March 13, 1837, report detailed the painstaking efforts of Seguin and the men of his battalion:

"I caused the honors of war to be paid to the remains of the Heroes of the Alamo on the 25th of Feby last. The ashes were found in three heaps. I caused a coffin to be prepared neatly covered with black, the ashes from the two smaller heaps were placed therein and with a view to attach additional solemnity to the occasion were carried to the Parish Church in Bexar whence it was moved with the procession at 4 o'clock in the afternoon of the day above mentioned. The Procession passed through the principal street of the city, crossed the River and passing through the principal avenue arrived at the spot whence part of the ashes had been collected, and the procession halted. The coffin was placed on the spot, and three volleys of musquetry were discharged over it by one of the companies, proceeding onward to the second spot from whence the ashes were taken where the same honors were done and thence to the principal spot and place of interment, the coffin was then placed upon a large heap of ashes where I addressed a few words to the Battalion and assemblage present in honor of the occasion in the Castillian language as I do not possess the English. Major Western then addressed the concourse in the latter tongue."

In his remarks to his battalion, Colonel Seguin ended: "Behold your brothers, Travis, Bowie, and Crockett as well as all the others. Their valor has earned them a place with all my heroes."

As with many questions about the Alamo and its defenders, there is no clear conclusion about the present location of the ashes of the defenders. A coffin in the San Fernando Church may contain their ashes. Some historians contend that the ashes were buried elsewhere, in a peach orchard somewhere near the Alamo.

Roy Sullivan

Lieutenant Colonel Juan Seguin of Texas: Commanded a Company during the San Jacinto Victory. Later Led His Battalion in Paying Final Homage to the Fallen Defenders of the Alamo. Credit N.K. Rogers photograph

# FOURTEEN

## DEFENDERS KILLED IN
## THE ALAMO (KIA)

T HE PRECEDING CHAPTERS have outlined the
bravery and valor of the Alamo defenders. The first roster
of the soldiers sacrificing their lives in the defense of the Alamo
appeared in the March 24, 1836, issue of the Telegraph and
Texas Register. It contained 115 names.

The roster has been revised numerous times, each with a
higher number of names due to painstaking research by several
historians.

The following roster contains 212 names. It is not intended
to be the last such roster of fallen heroes, as historical research
continues.

This is not an appendix of additional information. It is the
substance of this work.

| RANK | NAME | ORIGIN |
| --- | --- | --- |
| Sergeant | Abamillo, Juan | Texas |
| Private | Allen, Robert. | Virginia |
| Soldier | Andrews, George | Unknown |
| Private | Andross, Miles D. | Vermont |
| Private | Autry, Micajah North | Carolina |
| Sergeant | Badillo, Juan A. | Texas |

Roy Sullivan

| | | |
|---|---|---|
| Private | Bailey, Peter J. III | Kentucky |
| Private | Baker, Isaac G. | Arkansas |
| Captain | Baker, William C.M. | Missouri |
| Soldier | Ballard, John | Unknown |
| Private | Ballentine, John J. | Pennsylvania |
| Private | Ballentine, Richard W. | Scotland |
| Captain | Baugh, John J. | Virginia |
| Private | . Bayless, Joseph | Tennessee |
| Private | Blair, John | Tennessee |
| Captain | Blair, Samuel | Tennessee |
| Captain | Blazeby, William | England |
| Second Lieutenant | Bonham, James B. | South Carolina |
| Private | Bourne, Daniel | England |
| Colonel | Bowie, James | Kentucky |
| Soldier | Bowman, J.B. | Unknown |
| Private | Buchanan, James | Alabama |
| Private | Burns, Samuel E. | Ireland |
| Private | Butler, George D. | Missouri |
| Private | Cain, John | Pennslyania |
| Lieutenant | Campbell, Robert | Tennessee |
| Captain | Carey, William R. | Virginia |
| Private | Clark, M.B. | Mississippi |
| Private | Cloud, Daniel W. | Kentucky |
| Private | Cochran, Robert E. | New Hampshire |
| Lieutenant | Cottle, George W. | Missouri |
| Private | Courtman, Henry | Germany |
| Private | Crawford, Lemuel South | Carolina |
| Colonel | Crockett, David | Tennessee |

| | | |
|---|---|---|
| Private | Crossman, Robert | Pennsylvania |
| Private | Cummings, David P. | Pennsylvania |
| Private | Cunningham, Robert | New York |
| Lieutenant | Darst, Jacob C. | Kentucky |
| Private | Davis, John | Kentucky |
| Private | Day, Freeman H.K. | Unknown |
| Private | Daymon, Squire | Tennessee |
| Private | Dearduff, William | Tennessee |
| Soldier | Debichi, N. | Unknown |
| Private | Dennison, Stephen | England/Ireland |
| Soldier | Desauque, John | Louisiana |
| Private | Despallier, Charles | Louisiana |
| Private | Dewall Lewis | New York |
| Captain | Dickinson, Almaron | Tennessee |
| Soldier | Dickson, James | Unknown |
| Private | Dillard, John H. | Tennessee |
| Sergeant | Dimpkins, James R. | England |
| Private | Duvalt, Andrew | Ireland |
| Soldier | Edwards, Samuel M. | Unknown |
| Soldier | Eigenauer, Conrad | Unknown |
| Soldier | Elliott, J.D. | Unknown |
| Soldier | Elm, Frederick E. | Unknown |
| Private | Espalier, Carlos | Texas |
| Private | Esparza, Jose G. | Texas |
| Major | Evans, Robert | Ireland |
| Private | Evans, Samuel B. | New York |
| Private | Ewing, James L. | Tennessee |
| Private | Fauntleroy, William K. | Kentucky |

| | | |
|---|---|---|
| Private | Fishbaugh, William | Alabama |
| Private | Flanders, John | New Hampshire |
| Private | Floyd, Dolphin W. | North Carolina |
| Captain | Forsyth, John H. | New York |
| Private | Fuentes, Antonio | Texas |
| Private | Fuqua, Galba | Alabama |
| Private | Garnett, William | Virginia |
| Private | Garrand, James W. | Louisiana |
| Private | Garrett, James G. | Tennessee |
| Private | Garvin, John E. | Unknown |
| Private | Gaston, John E. | Unknown |
| Private | George, James | Unknown |
| Soldier | George, William | Unknown |
| Soldier | Gibson, James | Unknown |
| Third Lieutenant | Goodrich, John C. | Virginia |
| Private | Gray, Francis H. | Unknown |
| Private | Green, W.T. | Unknown |
| Private | Grimes, Albert C. | Georgia |
| Private | Gwin, James C. | England |
| Private | Harris, John | Kentucky |
| Private | Harrison, Andrew J. | Tennessee |
| Soldier | Harrison, I.L.K. | Unknown |
| Captain | Harrison, William B. | Ohio |
| Private | Hawkins, Joseph M. | Ireland |
| Private | Hays, John M. | Tennessee |
| Private | Heiskell, Charles M. | Tennessee |
| Private | Herndon, Patrick H. | Virginia |
| Sergeant | Hersee, William D. | England |

| | | |
|---|---|---|
| Private | Holland, Tapley | Ohio |
| Soldier | Holloway, James | Unknown |
| Private | Holloway, Samuel | Pennsylvania |
| Soldier | Howell, William D. | Massachusetts |
| Soldier | Hunter, William | Unknown |
| Soldier | Hutchinson, Thomas P. | Unknown |
| Soldier | Irwin, William A. | Unknown |
| Private | Jackson Thomas R. | Ireland |
| Lieutenant | Jackson, William D. | Kentucky |
| Major | Jameson, Green B. | Kentucky |
| Corporal | Jennings, Gordon C. | Connecticut |
| Private | Jimenez, Damacio | Texas |
| Private | Johnson, Lewis | Illinois |
| Private | Johnson, William | Pennsylvania |
| Lieutenant | Jones, John | New York |
| Private | Kenny, James | Virginia |
| Private | Kent, Andrew | Virginia |
| Soldier | Kent, Joseph | Unknown |
| Private | Kerr, Joseph | Louisiana |
| Lieutenant | Kimble, George C. | Pennsylvania |
| Private | Kin, John C. | Unknown |
| Private | King, William P. | Mississippi |
| Private | Lewis, William I. | Virginia |
| 3dCorporal | Lightfoot, William J. | Kentucky |
| Private | Lindley, Jonathan | Illinois |
| Private | Linn, William | Massachusetts |
| Private | Losoya, Toribio | Texas |
| Lieutenant | Main, George W. | Virginia |

Roy Sullivan

| | | |
|---|---|---|
| Prvate | Malone, William T. | Georgia |
| Private | Marshall, William | Tennessee |
| Captain | Martin, Albert | Rhode Island |
| Lieutenant | McCafferty, Edward | Unknown |
| Soldier | McClelland, Ross | Unknown |
| Soldier | McCoy, Daniel, Jr. | Unknown |
| Private | McCoy, Jesse | Tennessee |
| Soldier | McCoy, Prospect | Unknown |
| Private | McDowell, William | Pennsylvania |
| Private | McGee, James | Ireland |
| Sergeant | McGregor, John | Scotland |
| Private | McKinney, Robert | Ireland |
| Soldier | McNeilly, S.W. | Unknown |
| Lieutenant | Melton, Eliel | Georgia |
| Private | Miller, Thomas R. | Tennessee |
| Private | Mills, William | Tennessee |
| Private | Millsaps, Isaac | Mississippi |
| Soldier | Mitchasson, Edward F. | Virginia |
| Private | Mitchell, Edwin T. | Unknown |
| Private | Mitchell, Napoleon B. | Unknown |
| Private | Moore, Robert B. | Virginia |
| Private | Moore, Willis A. | Unknown |
| Soldier | Morman, John | Unknown |
| Soldier | Morrison, William | Unknown |
| Sergeant | Musselman, Robert | Ohio |
| Soldier | Nash, James | Unknown |
| Sergeant | Nava, Andres | Texas |
| Private | Neggan, George | S.Carolina |

| | | |
|---|---|---|
| Private | Nelson, Andrew M. | Tennessee |
| Private | Nelson, Edward | S.Carolina |
| Private | Nelson, George | S.Carolina |
| Private | Northcross, James | Virginia |
| Private | Nowlan, James | England |
| Soldier | O'Neil, L.R. | Unknown |
| Private | Olamio, George | Ireland |
| Private | Pagan, George | Unknown |
| Private | Parker, Christopher A. | Unknown |
| Private | Parks, William | N.Carolina |
| Private | Perry, Richardson | Mississippi |
| Soldier | Petrasweiz, Adolph | Unknown |
| Soldier | Pollard, Amos | Massachusetts |
| Private | Reynolds, John P. | Pennsylvania |
| Private | Roberts, Thomas H. | Unknown |
| Private | Robertson, James W. | Tennessee |
| Soldier | Rodriguez, Guadalupe | Unknown |
| Private | Rose, James M. | Ohio |
| Major | Roth, Jacob | Unknown |
| Private | Rusk, Jackson J. | Ireland |
| Private | Rutherford, Joseph | Kentucky |
| Private | Ryan, Isaac | Louisiana |
| Soldier | Sanders, W.H. | Unknown |
| Private | Scurlock, Mial | N.Carolina |
| Private | Sewell, Marcus L. | England |
| Private | Shied, Manson | Georgia |
| Lieutenant | Simmons, Cleveland K. | S.Carolina |
| Private | Smith, Andrew H. | Tennessee |

Roy Sullivan

| | | |
|---|---|---|
| Private | Smith, Charles S. | Maryland |
| Sergeant | Smith, Joshua G. | N.Carolina |
| Private | Smith, William H. | Unknown |
| Private | Spratt, John | Unknown |
| Private | Starr, Richard | England |
| Private | Stewart, James E. | England |
| Private | Stockton, Richard L. | New Jersey |
| Private | Summerlin, A. Spain | Tennessee |
| Private | Summers, William E. | Tennessee |
| Private | Sutherland, William D. | Alabama |
| Private | Taylor, Edward | Tennessee |
| Private | Taylor, George | Tennessee |
| Private | Taylor, James | Tennessee |
| Private | Taylor, William | Tennessee |
| Private | Thomas, B.Archer M. | Tennessee |
| Private | Thomas, Henry | Germany |
| Soldier | Thompson | Unknown |
| Private | Thomson, John W. | N.Carolina |
| Second Lieutenant | Thurston, John M. | Pennsylvania |
| Private | Trammel, Burke | Ireland |
| Lieutenant Colonel | Travis, William B. | S.Carolina |
| Private | Tumlinson, George W. | Missouri |
| Private | Tylee, James J. | New York |
| Private | Walker, Asa | Tennessee |
| Private | Walker, Jacob | Tennessee |
| Sergeant | Ward, William B. | Ireland |
| Private | Washington, Joseph G. | Tennessee |

| | | |
|---|---|---|
| Private | Waters, Thomas | England |
| Private | Wells, William | Georgia |
| Sergeant | White, Isaac | Unknown |
| Captain | White, Robert | England |
| Sgt. Major | Williamson, H. J. | Penn. |
| Soldier | Wills, William | Unknown |
| Private | Wilson, David L. | Scotland |
| Private | Wilson, John | Penn. |
| Private | Wolf, Anthony | Unknown |
| Private | Wright, Claiborne | N.Carolina |
| Lieutenant | Zanco, Charles | Denmark |

# FIFTEEN

## HOUSTON LEARNS OF THE MASSACRE AND ACTS

AS THE BATTLE ended on March 6, Susannah Dickinson was led to Santa Ana for interview. On arrival she found her daughter Angelina sitting on the Mexican general's lap. Colonel Almonte, aide-de-camp to Santa Ana, interpreted their conversation.

Santa Ana wanted to adopt Angelina, take her to Mexico City and raise her as his daughter. Susannah objected in no uncertain terms, despite being his prisoner at the moment. Santa Ana eventually relented and released them.

Susannah, Angelina and Joe, Travis's servant, and Ben, a courier of Santa Ana's, were escorted to the Gonzales road on March 13. On the way to Gonzales they encountered Deaf Smith, a scout for Sam Houston, seeking news of the Alamo.

Together, they hurried to Gonzales to tell General Houston the tragic news that the Alamo had fallen and all defenders killed. Once in Gonzales and identified as Alamo survivors, Susannah and Angelina were hurried to Houston's tent.

Once seated there, Susannah's leg wound was treated. Houston sat down beside them to hear their sad news of the fall of the Alamo.

"They were all killed?" Houston repeated.

"Yes," an anguished Susannah answered. "All killed."

At this Houston wept openly as the two females were escorted out of his tent.

He had been named by the Texas Convention meeting at Washington-on-the-Brazos as the Commander-in-Chief of the Texas army being formed from the hundred or so volunteers gathering in Gonzales.

Houston's immediate tasks were daunting: warn the colonists' settlements and the Convention of the Mexican danger while attempting to organize, train, equip and provision his new army.

Were that not enough, he had to evade Santa Ana's forces until Houston's tiny army was capable of operating against a much larger, better equipped, seasoned

Mexican military.

The threat to civilian settlers throughout East Texas was real and immediate. Santa Ana even spelled out his intentions in a proclamation delivered by Ben, his courier. In part, the proclamation warned:

"I am pained to find amongst those adventurers (meaning rebels) the names of some colonists, to whom have been granted repeated benefits, and who had no just motive of complaint against the government of their adopted country. These ungrateful men must also suffer the just punishment that the laws and public vengeance demand."

Houston acted quickly. Within hours, he led his volunteers and the remaining populace of Gonzales out of town, which he burned on the way out. The rest of East Texas scrambled to follow to escape the advancing Mexican army wreaking, as ordered, "punishment and vengeance." This panicky migration was called the "Runway Scrape."

# SIXTEEN
## WHAT HAPPENED TO MONSTER SANTA ANA?

**G**ENERAL HOUSTON'S RAGGED Texas army fled eastward, closely followed by the Mexicans. Near present day Houston, Texas, in a bayou called San Jacinto, General Houston finally ordered his scrappy, unhappy troops to attack the Mexican positions at midday.

The date was April 21, 1836. The Mexicans were napping.

"Remember the Alamo!" the Texans screamed at the surprised, thoroughly frightened soldiers of Santa Ana.

Among the Texas victors, happy to be fighting instead of retreating, was the Tejano Company commanded by Captain Juan Seguin, part of the Second Texas Regiment.

Santa Ana may have been napping, too, at the moment of the Texas surprise assault. Legend portrays him as entertaining Emily West, the fabled "Yellow Rose of Texas," in his silken tent. The next day a bedraggled Mexican General-in-Chief was captured in a swamp, wearing the uniform of a private.

By later signing the Treaty of Velasco with the Texas President, David G. Burnet, Santa Ana acknowledged the independence of the Republic of Texas and ordered the Mexican army to withdraw back to Mexico. In return, Burnet promised Santa Ana his eventual safe return to Vera Cruz, Mexico.

On his circuitous way to Vera Cruz, Santa Ana met with U.S. President Jackson in Washngton, D.C., in 1837. Perhaps the two compared experiences. Jackson had brutally treated Native Americans. Santa Ana exceeded Jackson by his excesses against the people of the state of Zacatecas and the defenders of the Alamo. Santa Ana was returned to Vera Cruz in style, aboard a U.S.Navy ship.

In 1838 Mexico was losing another war, this one the "Pastry War" with France. Santa Ana was reinstated by his government as its army commander tasked with defeating the French. At Vera Cruz, his army was routed and Santa Ana wounded so severely his leg was amputated. The leg was buried with full military honors and war hero Santa Ana reentered politics.

The government headed by President Bustamante proved ineffective and Santa Ana was asked to return to office. Unbelievably, he was inaugurated as Mexico's president for the fifth time.

Taking to the field with the army, Santa Ana defeated a rebel army headed by two generals, Urrea and Mexia.

In 1842 Santa Ana attempted to retake Texas, but failed. The next year he was unable to restore the treasury by raising taxes. His tax increases were so unpopular that several states ignored the central government. The state of Yucatan even declared its independence. Evading capture, Santa Ana returned home to Vera Cruz but was captured and exiled to Cuba.

When the U.S. declared war on Mexico in 1846, Santa Ana again volunteered his services to save Mexico. He declared himself Presidente and assumed dictatorial control of the government. By 1848 the U.S. defeated Mexico and Santa Ana was again exiled, this time to Kingston, Jamaica.

In exchange for agreeing to restore the properties of the Catholic Church, Santa Ana again assumed the office of president in 1853. He was no more successful than before but increased his personal finances and declared himself "dictator for life" with the imposing title "Most Serene Highness."

In 1854 he was removed from office under the Plan of

Ayutla and exiled again. His hopes of returning to power were thwarted by the rebellion led by Benito Juarez. He returned to Cuba, was tried in absentia in Mexico and found guilty.

Until 1874 Santa Ana lived in Cuba, the U.S., Colombia and St. Thomas. That year a general amnesty was declared by the Mexican government, so Santa Ana returned to Mexico. Infirm, almost blind and now impoverished, he is remembered as the man who was President or Vice President of Mexico eleven times but who also lost half of Mexico's territory, an estimated one million square miles.

His Mexico City obituary was brief:

"General Antonio Lopez de Santa Ana died in this City on the 21$^{st}$ inst. However he may be condemned by parties, his career formed a brilliant and important portion of the History of Mexico and future historians will differ in their judgment of his merit. General Santa Ana outlived his usefulness and ambition and died at the ripe age of eighty-four.

Peace to his ashes." (note: Santa Ana was eighty-two, not eighty-four, at the time of his death).

# RECOMMENDED READING

Baugh, Virgil E. "Rendevous at the Alamo," Lincoln, Nebraska: University of braska Press, 1960.

Becerra, Francisco. "A Mexican Sergeant's Recollections of the Alamo and San Jacinto," Austin, Texas: Jenkins Publishing Company, 1980.

Bonham,William N. "James Butler Bonham, Messenger of Defeat," Austin, Texas: Langmere Publishing Company, 2003.

Davis, William C. "Three Roads to the Alam," New York, NY: Harper Collins Publishing Company, 1998.

De la Pena, Jose Enrique. "With Santa Ana in Texas: A Personal Narrative of the Revolution," College Station, Texas, Texas A&M University Press, 1975.

Groneman, Bill, "Alamo Defenders," Austin, Texas: Eakin Press, 1990.

Groneman, Bill, "Death of a Legend," Plano, Texas: Republic of Texas Press,1999

Groneman, Bill, "Eyewitness to the Alamo,: Plano, Texas: Republc of Texas Press, 2001.

Lord, Walter, "A Time to Stand," Lincoln, Nebraska: University of Nebraska Press, 1961.

Procter, Ben, "Heroes of Texas," Waco, Texas: The Texian Press, 1966.

Wikipedia, "List of Alamo Defenders"

Printed in the United States
By Bookmasters